Women
of the
Twelfth Century

Women
of the
Twelfth Century

Volume Three:
Eve and the Church

Georges Duby

Translated by Jean Birrell

The University of Chicago Press

GEORGES DUBY was a member of the Académie Française, and taught for many years at the Collège de France. Of his many books, five have been published in translation by the University of Chicago Press: *The Three Orders; The Age of the Cathedrals; The Knight, the Lady, and the Priest; History Continues;* and *Love and Marriage in the Middle Ages.* The University of Chicago Press and Polity Press are publishing *Women of the Twelfth Century,* in three volumes.

The University of Chicago Press, Chicago 60637
Polity Press, Cambridge CB2 1UR, UK
This English translation © Polity Press and The University of Chicago 1998
All rights reserved. Published 1998
Printed in Great Britain
07 06 05 04 03 02 01 00 99 98   1 2 3 4 5 6

ISBN: 0–226–16785–2 (cloth)
ISBN: 0–226–16786–0 (paper)

First published in French as *Dames du XIIe Siècle, III: Ève et les prêtres,* © Éditions Gallimard, 1996.
First published in English in 1998 by the University of Chicago Press and by Polity Press in association with Blackwell Publishers Ltd.

Published with the assistance of the French Ministry of Culture.

Library of Congress Cataloging-in-Publication Data

Duby, Georges.
    [Dames du XIIème siècle. English]
    Women of the twelfth century / Georges Duby : translated by Jean Birrell.
        p. cm.
    Contents: v. 1. Eleanor of Aquitaine and six others.
    ISBN 0–226–16776–0 (cloth : v. 1 : alk. paper).—ISBN 0–226–16780–1 (pbk. : v. 1 : alk. paper)
    1. Women—France—History—Middle Ages, 500–1500. 2. Women—France—Biography. I. Title.
HQ1147.F7D813 1997
305.4′ 0944′ 0902—DC21   97–14198
                                                                                               CIP

This book is printed on acid-free paper.

Contents

Introduction

During the twelfth century, the Western Church at last turned its attention to the expectations of women, who felt they were neglected and who were calling for more assistance in their progress towards salvation. Of course, the great prelates who had spearheaded the moral reform of Christian society in the previous century had realized that it was necessary to be concerned with women as well as men, and to dissuade them from evil; the most open-minded men of prayer, those most receptive to the teaching of the Gospels, had already gathered around them women who were especially anxious or needy. But the ecclesiastical authorities distrusted these rash apostles. Disappointed, many women listened to the heretics, who were reaching out to them. It soon became urgent to protect them against the attractions of the sects and to bring the lost sheep back into the fold. Priests then began to talk more about women. Some spoke to women; sometimes they listened to them. Traces of their words survive, and they shed a little light on what I am seeking to discover, and is so hard to see, that is, how women were treated at this period.

I am under no illusion, as I am well aware that what these churchmen wrote no more reveals the actual reality of women's daily lives than do the sources I have used in the previous volumes. It is men who are speaking, trapped in their male prejudices and obliged, furthermore, by the discipline of their order to keep well away from women and to fear them. In this book, too, I will capture only images, flickering and imperfect reflections, of the women of the twelfth century. I turn to this evidence, nevertheless, for want of any better, for the final, vital stage of my project.

1

The Sins of Women

S tephen of Fougères had been a chaplain of Henry
Plantagenet, one of those priests who conducted the
services for the princely household. He had served his
powerful master so well that, in 1168, he became bishop of
Rennes. He was a good and conscientious bishop. In order
to guide men towards what was good, especially the men of
the Church, for whom chastity was obligatory, and who
must be encouraged to fight against their lust, he wrote lives
of saints in Latin, in particular that of William Firmat, an
example of the renunciation of the joys of the flesh. Firmat
had lived in the area in the previous century. He, too, had
been a priest, and he had become rich through teaching, like
Abelard. Then, touched by grace, he had chosen to end his
days as a hermit, in poverty and abstinence. The devil set a
trap for him. To escape the attentions of overzealous disciples, the ascetic had retreated deep into the woods. It was
there that some evil-minded young men devised a way of
throwing a girl into his arms. One evening, she came
knocking on the door of his retreat: 'Open up', she said. 'I'm
frightened, the wild animals are going to eat me.' William
took her in, fanned the embers of his fire and offered her
some bread. She, in return, deployed her charms. The 'iron
man' took up the challenge. Satan attacked him with the fires
of lust; he counter-attacked with natural fire. With a brand,

he burned deep into his flesh, to the wonder of the 'whore', who repented. It was a victory over the self and over lechery, but also a victory over female power, and over the danger that stems from women. For Stephen, women were bearers of evil. He repeated this forcefully in the *Book of Manners*, composed between 1174 and 1178. He wrote it in the Romance dialect, so it was aimed at the people of the court, at knights and ladies.

This long poem – 336 stanzas, 1,344 verses – is a sermon in palatable form. Or rather it is a collection of six sermons, each dealing with one social category, emphasizing its specific failings and offering it a model of conduct. For in the last quarter of the twelfth century, conscious of the complexity of society, preachers thought it wise to speak in a tone appropriate to the various 'estates' which composed it. The oversimplified image of a perfect society, conforming to the plan of the Creator, that is, the image of the three orders, priests, warriors and workers, called on to assist each other, may still occupy the centre of the work, where two exactly balanced parts meet. But before this, the author spoke of the rulers – kings, clergy and knights – and afterwards, he moved on to the ruled – peasants, burgesses and, lastly, women. For the first time in what survives today of the literature in secular language, woman are shown as forming an *ordo*, endowed with its own morality and subject to its own failings. These are denounced with great ferocity and verve.

Stephen did not discuss all women. His duties required him to pay particular attention to the upper levels of society, to the rulers and the noble houses, and it was to the nobility and not to ordinary people that he spoke. He focused his gaze, therefore, on the women who were to be found in the great houses, 'the matrons and the young ladies,/the chambermaids and the maidservants', and when he came to describe female sins, it was married women alone whom he castigated. Queening it alongside their husbands in the great hall, he says, neither spinning nor weaving (as the beguines did at this period, and as St Godeliva did, to escape temptation), doing nothing, idle, they were, first and foremost, more exposed than other women to sin. It was right that they should be the first to be reprimanded because, in the prominent position they occupied, they were watched and imitated and there was a risk that, through them, sin might be spread. Furthermore, the consequences of the disorders provoked by their lapses were more serious. Married women 'sowed hatreds', they were 'seeds of war'.

This judgemental churchman found three major vices in the female nature. According to him, women were prone to deflecting the course of events, hence to opposing divine intentions, by the use of practices, most of them culinary, whose secrets they passed on to each other. They were all sorceresses to a degree, and together they concocted suspect mixtures, starting with the make-up, unguents and depilatory creams to which they resorted, misrepresenting their physical appearance in order to deceive men: 'Whores make themselves virgins/and the ugly and the wrinkled become beauties.' It was commonplace at this period, among men of the Church, to condemn cosmetics. They were displeasing to God, who, it was well known, forbade people to deform the human body that He had made with His own hands; when they were painted 'in white or in red', He did not recognize his creatures. Thus far, however, the sin was venial. It became much more serious when women made and dispensed preparations intended to prevent conception or procure abortion, 'to kill the child inside their daughters/who had carelessly got pregnant'. Last, there was the horrible sin of those who went so far as to bewitch men, trying to control them by incantations and spells or by the dolls they had learned to fashion from wax or clay, or who tried to make them waste away by 'poisoning [them] with bad herbs', in fact, to kill them. Their prime target was, of course, their husband, their 'lord'.

For, and this was their second failing, women were intractable and aggressive, naturally hostile to the man to whom their father or brother or eldest son had given them. They would not tolerate the necessary supervision. Thus, between the conjugal couple, there was perpetual, veiled, stubborn and cruel war. Before the husband who got angry when he found her so distant when he wanted to make love, the wife became ever more 'obtuse', more 'stubborn', 'morose' and – Stephen, as a connoisseur, chose his words with care – 'mute'. Women were rebels, women were treacherous, they were vindictive and their first revenge was to take a lover.

In fact, the third defect from which their nature suffered – and here we get to the heart of what was malign in them – had at this period, in this language, a name: *lécherie*: lust. Women were consumed by a desire that, feeble creatures that they were, they could not control. It led them straight into adultery. When their husband needed them, they froze up, suppressing their ardour. But, unsatisfied, they ran after attractive men. They did this anywhere. In shadowy churches, where the nocturnal offices were propitious to furtive encounters (according to Guibert of Nogent, Count John of Soissons 'liked to ogle pretty women there'), women were to be seen on the lookout, casting about in search of pleasure. If they had no luck, in default of a partner of good blood, they made do with the menservants, forcing them to have sex with them as if they were bitches on heat. Lastly, the fire which consumed them led on into the 'ugly sin', the sin 'against nature', the most execrable sin of all. On this subject, the bishop let rip. His diatribe ends with a collection of dirty jokes. In twenty verses, in more than a dozen metaphors borrowed from the language of the joust, and of fencing, fishing and milling, he suggests twists and turns in the 'game that women have discovered'. In a torrent, all the *double entendres* which so delighted the knights when, among themselves, they imagined all the things they claimed that women liked to do with other women, pour out. One can almost hear the guffaws of the audience.

Stephen of Fougères was clever. The better to instruct his flock, he set out to amuse them. In fact, he was in deadly earnest. Behind the frivolity and the sarcasms lies a strong warning, and it is entirely based on an idea that was never questioned, that was not even open to question, the idea of women formed by the rulers of the Church in twelfth-century France. They laid it on the line. Nature, they believed, had dug a deep ditch between two distinct species, the male and the female. This fracture was the front in an implacable battle. It was women who attacked, brandishing the arms of the weak and the stubborn. Nevertheless, as they struggled to control their own appetites, the priests put at the root of this evil, at the source of all the wickedness of women, the raging sensuality that they believed naturally consumed them.

Stephen invented nothing, except greatly to increase the number of the ribald terms that make his virulent discourse so powerful. He took his place in a large and a very ancient tradition of misogynous writing. He remembered the Latin authors who were discussed in his day by the masters of grammar and rhetoric in the schools of the Loire Valley; he remembered Ovid, the Sixth Satire of Juvenal and St Jerome. Nevertheless, what he expressed with such verve was not simply a tissue of commonplaces drawn from the classical authors of Roman Antiquity. Fully accepted in courtly circles, he certainly spoke from experience. But to compose his thirty-eight stanzas vituperating women, and to meet the expectations of the courtly audience, he adapted and transposed the contents of ecclesiastical libraries into the language of chivalric diversions, like so many learned men at this period, like the authors of the *Roman de Troie* and of the bestiaries and the lapidaries, and like the 'scholars' patronized by Count Baldwin of Guînes. And above all, he drew directly on two works he found close at hand, in the book-cupboard of the episcopal residence. The first was the *Book of Ten Chapters*, written half a century earlier by Marbode, one of his predecessors as bishop of Rennes. Marbode, discussing 'the prostitute', had painted, in eighty strongly worded verses, a terrible picture of women. They had already shown themselves to be enemies of 'the male gender', spreading their nets wide, provoking scandals, brawls and plots. They were treacherous, like Eve: 'Who was it who had argued for tasting what was forbidden?' They were quarrelsome, greedy, frivolous and jealous and, crowning this accumulation of evils, was a voracious womb. Marbode here took up again the image of the ancient chimera: a head, that of a lion, Medusa-like and carnivorous, and a tail, that of a

dragon, deceiving, sowing death and damnation. Between
the two, however, he put, not the body of a horse, but a
furnace: fire, incandescence, combustion, devouring. Let no
one dare to confront this monster, whose blows could not be
parried; run away, as fast as your legs will carry you.

The *Book of Ten Chapters*, like the *Book of Manners*, was
a stylistic exercise. In the twelfth century, the prelates of
these regions were very fond of displaying their literary
expertise in poems of this type, precious and elaborate. The
other work from which the moral lesson delivered by Stephen
of Fougères is derived, and much more directly, is very
different. It, too, was the work of a bishop, Burchard of
Worms. But this is an austere treatise, a practical administrative manual, a 'canonical collection', in the phrase of the
scholars. It was called the *Decretum*. It showed where the
law was to be found, bringing together and classifying the
'canons', the decisions taken over the course of time in
councils, the assemblies of bishops, and the prescripts contained in the books called 'penitentials' because they
recorded, for each fault, the penalty that was supposed to
redeem it. Inventories of this type had been composed for
some decades. They helped the leaders of the Church to
perform one of their main functions, to judge and to define
offences, drawing on the authority of their predecessors, in
order to suppress them and, in so doing, gradually to
establish the solid rules of a morality. Between 1007 and
1012, the bishop of Worms had set to work. At this period,
and in a region, Greater Lorraine, between Metz and
Cologne, spared by the last pagan invasions, where the cult
of Mary Magdalen, the penitent, was increasing in popularity
and where a high culture in direct and uninterrupted line
of descent from Carolingian traditions was flourishing, the
purging of the episcopal body was gathering pace. The
prelates had been chosen with care and were now setting out
to reform the morals of their flocks. Burchard collected
references, put them in a convenient order, and constructed
his *Decretum* for his own use and for the use of his friends.
He had been a monk at Lobbes. One of his old masters, now
bishop of Gembloux, and the bishop of Speyer came to his

assistance. When one considers the very crude tools then available to scholars, if only to fix words by writing them down, one can only marvel at the scale of the work accomplished. Its vigour and its clarity are amazing. It was admired and it was copied throughout the dioceses of the Empire and northern France. In this part of Christendom, it was used by every bishop during the eleventh and up to the end of the twelfth centuries to uncover sin and to dispense redemptive punishments equitably.

The *Decretum* is presented as the indispensable tool of a general purification. Of its twenty books, the first five deal with the clergy and the sacraments they distribute, that is, with the agents of this necessary cleansing. Next comes a reasoned catalogue of the sins that must be extirpated by being punished according to their gravity. They are ranked in a logical order, which leads from the public faults to the most private, beginning, in Book VI, with murder and ending, in Book XVII, with fornication. Book XX, the *Liber speculationum*, is a meditation on man's last days, on death and what comes after. The preceding book, which is entirely devoted to penitence, is 'called *Corrector* or *Medicus* because it contains the corrections of the body and the medicines of the soul and because it teaches priests, even the simplest, how to bring relief to every person, rich or poor, a child, young or old, decrepit, healthy, infirm, of all ages and of both sexes'. It is a recapitulation, a sort of summary, which, since it was more manageable, was much more widely distributed than the treatise as a whole. It was easy to find there, for each sin, the precise tariff of the public penance that it was proper for the bishop or his delegates to impose. The *Corrector* is therefore a penitential, the last and greatest, the high point of the genre. But it is more than this, because it claims not only to correct but to treat. 'Medicine of the soul', it attacks evil in embryo, and was less useful therefore to the judges who passed sentence than to the inquisitor whose task was to search out the guilty. In fact, the list of sanctions appears simply as the supplement to an interrogation. For, in the eleventh century, the ways of administering the sacrament of penance were slowly becoming more com-

plex. Priests ought to help sinners to purge themselves
wholly, hence to put them to the question, to force them to
confess. As soon as penitents began to admit their faults,
they should be made to feel shame, and be pressed to go
further and to look clear-sightedly into the depths of their
soul. 'Perhaps, dearly beloved, everything that you have done
does not come to mind; I am going to question you and you
should take great care not to conceal anything at the instiga-
tion of the devil. And then he will question him, in order.' A
penitential in the old style, the *Corrector* is really a precursor
of the manuals that were beginning to be written at the end
of the twelfth century for the use of confessors.

Burchard, too, had a model. A hundred years earlier, in the
same region, Regino, once abbot of Prüm, now abbot of
Saint-Martin of Trier, at the request of Bishop Ratbod, who
had asked for guidance in his pastoral visits throughout the
diocese and in the sessions of the court of episcopal justice,
had written two books, the second of which, *De Ecclesiasticis
Disciplinis*, contains a questionnaire, an interrogation on sin.
Burchard found it so valuable that he transcribed it in its
entirety at the beginning of the *Decretum*, in the part devoted
to the powers of the bishop. Here, however, the questions are
posed quite differently. They are put not by the priest to the
repentant sinner, but by the bishop to seven men chosen from
each parish, seven men 'of mature years, of good morals and
truthful', on oath. They stand before the prelate, who admon-
ishes them: 'You are about to swear an oath not before a man
but before God, your Creator . . . Take care that you hide
nothing, and that you are not damned for the sins of others.'
Not for their own sins, but for those of others: they were not
expected to dig deep into their own consciences and confess
their own failings, but they must reveal everything that they
knew, or that they had seen or heard, of the faults committed
around them, in the community at large. The bishop questions
them: 'Has there been a murder in this parish? Or a parricide?
. . . Has there not been someone who dared to sing round the
church some of those evil songs that make people laugh?'
There are eighty-nine questions and they, too, progress from
the most obvious crimes, the crimes of blood by which the

population as a whole was sullied, to the most private sexual misdemeanours and minor manifestations of disrespect with regard to the sacred. It was an *inquisitio*, an inquisitional procedure of the type that was periodically conducted by the public authorities in order to restore and maintain the peace.

Such a document reveals the first stage in a movement of great importance in the history of our culture. At the beginning of the tenth century, the active element within the Church can be seen to be perfecting its procedures of control and domination. It was infiltrating and insinuating itself among the faithful through the intermediary of sworn emissaries who were charged, heeding 'neither love, nor fear, gratitude, nor family affection', eyes wide open, ears cocked, with detecting the least indications of what the Church defined as sin. By this means, it tightened its grip on the behaviour of the laity. It was a beginning. A century later, in Burchard's time, the tool had been much improved. The priest now engaged in a dialogue, face to face and in confidence, with the parishioner. The bishop had delegated to him his power to oversee and to punish, advising him 'to be very discreet, to distinguish between him who had publicly sinned and done public penance, and him who had sinned secretly and confessed to himself'. The Church was now able to regulate the most intimate behaviour. Extending its scrutiny far deeper than had been possible for the inquisitors of the tenth century, it annexed to its sphere thoughts and deeds that no one had previously regarded as culpable, and by naming and describing them it metamorphosed them into crimes; in this way, it infinitely expanded the field of anxiety, of that fear of hell that drove people into deference towards it. It was a major innovation, matched by a second which was no less weighty in its consequences: Burchard of Worms demanded that the priest question women directly. Having set out 148 questions, the *Medicus* advises: 'If the above questions are common to women and to men, the ones that follow are directed especially to women.'

The first of these comes in the continuation of the general interrogation. It concerns 'unbelief'.

Have you done what some women are in the habit of doing at certain times of year? Have you prepared the table, the food and the drink in your house and placed three knives on the table so that the three sisters, whom the ancients called Fates, might perhaps eat something? Have you in this way taken away some of its power from the goodness of God and from His name to give it to the devil? Have you believed that the three sisters, as you call them, might be useful to you now or later?

The interrogation then comes to the crux, the female sin par excellence, lust, the quest for pleasure. Five questions in succession deal with the pleasure that women enjoy apart from men, in the privacy of the 'ladies' chamber'. The *Decretum* is not, like the *Book of Manners*, an amusing sermon. This cold work does not go in for circumlocutions. It calls a spade a spade and it gets straight to the point. 'Have you made what some women are in the habit of making, have you made a certain machine [*machinamentum*: in classical Latin, the word indicated the engines of attack employed by the Roman army, battering rams, ballistas or catapults] of the right size for you, have you bound it to the site of your sex or that of a woman friend and have you fornicated with other evil women, or others with you, with this instrument or with another?' Or had they used it 'to fornicate with themself?' Or had they done what those women do who, 'to assuage the desire that torments them join together as if they could marry'? 'Have you fornicated with your little boy, I mean to say, have you placed him on your sex and in this way imitated fornication?' 'Have you given yourself to an animal, have you by some trick aroused it to coitus?' A little further on, the confessor returns once again to pleasure, the more licit pleasure between spouses. Did not women, who were never satisfied, do their best wickedly to intensify it by employing a variety of procedures to stoke up the fires of their husband. 'Have you eaten the semen of your husband to make him burn more strongly with love for you?' Had they, to the same end, mixed diabolical and repugnant aphrodisiacs into what he had drunk or what he had eaten, little fish that they had marinated in their lap, or bread whose dough had been kneaded on their bare buttocks, or a little of their menstrual blood, or a pinch of ashes from a roasted testicle? Lastly, was it not in the nature of women to promote debauchery and to derive not only pleasure but profit from the use of their sex? 'Have you acted as a madam, for yourself or for others? I mean to say, have you, like the whores, sold your body to lovers for them to enjoy? Or, what is even more wicked and culpable, the body of another woman, I mean your daughter or your granddaughter, or another Christian woman? Or have you rented them out? Have you been a procuress?'

Just as women trifled with their bodies, so they trifled with death, in particular with that of their children. Already by the seventh question, the confessor is asking about this: 'Have you done what some women are in the habit of doing, when they have fornicated and when they wish to kill their offspring? They act to expel the foetus from the womb, either by evil spells or by herbs. Thus they kill and expel the foetus, or, if they have not yet conceived, they do what is necessary in order not to conceive.' Nevertheless, the 'doctor of the soul', wiser than Regino of Prüm, advises making a clear distinction: 'Is it because of poverty or because of the difficulty of feeding the child, or because of fornication and in order to conceal the sin?' Similarly, he regards the fault as less grave if the embryo was destroyed before it had 'quick-ened', before it had 'received the spirit', or been felt to move. More culpable, on the other hand, was the woman who taught a friend how to do it. Once born, the child was not out of danger. 'Have you deliberately killed your son or your daughter?' Or, 'negligent, have you let it die?' 'Have you left it too close to a cauldron of boiling water?' 'Have you smothered your child without meaning to by the weight of your clothes . . . Have you found it smothered beside you in the bed where you sleep with your husband? One cannot say whether it was smothered by the father or by you, or whether it died a natural death, but you ought not to be easy in your mind, or without repentance.' For women are often irresponsible, and it is their duty to 'watch over the child up to the age of seven'.

Up to this age, in fact, a woman's child belonged wholly to her, and not to men. It was her creature. Accordingly, she must be closely supervised. Women were prone to perform disquieting tricks with their children. When, for example, a child cried too loudly, the mother passed it through a hole, making a pretence, by means of this rite of passage, of exchanging it or of offering it to the evil powers in return for another, less difficult, child. But it was the way in which very young babies were buried that should particularly concern the priest. If they were stillborn or died without being baptized, had she 'driven a stake through their little body'? For if not, women said, 'they would rise from the dead and might harm many people'. If the child had died baptized, had someone 'put in their right hand a wax paten with a Host on it, or in the left hand a chalice containing wine'?

Their power over the dead and over death acknowledged, women were suspected of abusing it, engaged as they were in a ceaseless war against the other sex. Thus, the twelfth question asks: 'Have you concocted a deadly poison and killed a man with this poison? Or only wished to do so?' If not killed, they might at the very least have enfeebled men by spells, or destroyed their virility and generative faculties.

> Have you done what some adulterous women do? As soon as they learn that their lover is going to take a legitimate wife, they suppress his male desire by evil arts so that he will be impotent before his wife and unable to consummate their union . . . [Have you] coated your naked body with honey, put corn on a linen cloth on the ground, have you rolled all over in it, have you carefully collected all the grains stuck to your body, have you ground them, turning the mill widdershins, and have you made bread for your husband from this flour with the intention of making him die?

Or, in that fantasy in which the aggressiveness of women and their deep-seated hostility to the masculine species finds savage expression:

When you lie in your bed, your husband asleep on your breast, in the silence of the night, the doors closed, do you believe you can bodily go out, travel the earthly spaces with other women, victims of the same error, and kill without visible weapons men baptized and redeemed with the blood of Christ, then together eat their cooked flesh, put in place of their heart some straw or wood or other material and, having eaten them, make them live again, granting them as it were a truce?

Here, the confessor is attacking that final aspect of female perversity, sorcery, and question after question addresses nocturnal rides and tourneys, the wearing of the talismans that deflect the judgement of God and the spells by which women claimed to extend their power over the poultry, the milk and the honey of their neighbour, or influence the fate of another by enchantment. The questionnaire ends by describing a procession of little girls. A naked virgin leads them towards a stream; accompanied by the village matrons, she had earlier gone out to gather with the little finger of her right hand a sprig of henbane, and tied it to the little toe of her right foot; her companions sprinkle her with water, then return, taking one step forward and two steps back, 'like crayfish'. 'So, by their devilry, women hope to make it rain.' Earlier, various breaches of ecclesiastical discipline, of which women, thoughtless, talkative and careless, were frequently guilty, had been passed under review.

It is difficult to imagine Bishop Burchard breaching the impenetrable barrier that surrounded the female world and learning in person from old gossips the correct method for employing a dildo or the many recipes likely to arouse the ardour of men. In fact, he took his information from earlier texts and in particular from Regino of Prüm. Three-quarters of the forty-one questions had already appeared, differently formulated, in the latter's work.

When Abbot Regino imagined his bishop interrogating the seven men sworn to watch over the morals of the parish, all the questions he put into his mouth were in the masculine: 'Has there been a man (*aliquis*) who . . .?' He was well aware that the inquisitors would find it difficult to penetrate the enclosed domestic spaces within which women were cloistered, and that they would get most of their information from their more accessible neighbours, those whose activities took place in public, in the light of day: men. Nevertheless, the interrogation concerned both sexes ('Has there been a man or a woman (*aliqua*) . . .?') in the case of four categories of faults: recourse to spells ('Has anyone acted or taught how to act so that the husband cannot beget or the woman conceive?'), adultery, fornication and child neglect ('Has anyone smothered without meaning to their own child? Sick, has anyone left it to die without baptism?'). In eight instances, finally, women alone are presumed to be guilty of the offence. These are, first, four types of murder: abortion, of course; infanticide (the corpse of the child, a priori assumed to be the fruit of illicit sexual activity, is then supposed to have been hidden in the ground or in water); the murder of the husband 'by poisonous herbs or deadly drinks'; and the murder of a maidservant. The murder of a wife, we should note, was also punished, but only if the husband had been unable to prove that she had been of easy virtue. Also, it was the male head of the household who normally killed the male slaves, and the mistress the females, not, this time, using poison and insidiously, as to kill men, who were stronger than she was, but here using her hands, as in the case of newborn infants. It is clear that women disturbed men first of all because they were bearers of death. If a child died, before or after birth, it could only be the mother; if a husband was found dead in his bed in the morning, it could only be his wife, and by mysterious drugs, the recipes for which she knew. Next came sexuality. But here, only two of the twenty-one questions deal specifically with the behaviour of women: did they know any who abandoned their husband in favour of another man? or who sold their body or that of other women? Lastly, two of the sixteen questions in the fourth section, 'concerning enchanters and sorcerers', applied particularly to women. One is very general:

Is there a women who boasts of being able, by evil spell or incantation, to change men's minds, from hate to love or from love to hate, or to damage or steal away what belongs to men? And if any are found who say they ride out some nights in the company of a crowd of demons of female appearance ... she must be driven out of the parish by fair means or foul [imagine!].

The other fault was more an affair of working life: when they were weaving woollen or linen cloths, were they heard to be murmuring magic formulas? The way the questions formulated by Regino were apportioned between the two sexes shows that the idea that the nature of women led them to sin in a particular way was firmly entrenched at the beginning of the tenth century, a hundred years before Burchard of Worms set to work. Indeed, it came from further back still, since it was shared by the Carolingian clerks and monks who composed penitentials, including Theodore, Rabanus Maurus and Theodulf, bishop of Orleans. It was Burchard, however, who first sifted, picked out and set these sins apart and defined new ones.

Burchard divided the questions he found in Regino into two groups. In the first, he put those he called 'common to the two sexes'. We should not be misled by this; they are in fact addressed to men. He doubled the number of questions concerning sexuality and dealings with demonic forces. This is explicable in that the inquisitor was not here one of the parishioners but the priest, and he ought not to stop at what was evident, but, in the privacy of a dialogue with the penitent, push his enquiries much deeper, into more intimate matters, down into the most shadowy regions of the souls that it was his duty to care for and to subjugate. What is surprising is that he does not tell the priest to speak directly to women, given that no one doubted that they were paramount in the two fields of guilt, the sexual and the magical. His predecessors were familiar with the mistaken beliefs and bad practices they strove to extirpate, placed under the invocation of female powers, Diana, the sorceress Holda and 'those whom the foolish call the Fates'; they heard the incantations of women at funerals or as they performed their domestic duties, and they knew very well that it was female hands that tied the belts of the dead in a certain way in order to harm another, that broke wool-carding combs over the coffin and that threw pails of water under the stretcher before it left for the cemetery. Burchard knew this too, but it did not stop him from taking men to task. He may well not ask: 'Have you done such a thing?', since it was not men who acted. But he pressed them: 'Were you present? Did you allow it?' Have you heard women weavers murmuring magic formulas in the workshop in the gynaeceum? Have you believed that women are capable of transmuting into love the hatred of the man they covet, or of joining in diabolical night rides? Have you protested when they have performed round the catafalques the acts that the Church forbids? Do you believe that there are 'those wild women called sylphs who, people say, show themselves to their lovers when they will, take their pleasure with them, then hide and disappear? Do you believe that these fairies, when a child is born, can make of it what they will?' Similarly, everything concerning repudiation, adultery, fornication, sodomy and immodest caresses is in the masculine and, in the case of the prohibited sexual positions and of those times when it was forbidden 'to sleep together', it was the husband, and the husband alone, who was suspected of 'abusing his wife in this fashion'. But the conviction that women, perverted and excessively ardent, incited to sins of the flesh was nevertheless so powerful that once, though only once, a woman is shown taking the initiative: the sister of the wife who slipped surreptitiously into the marriage bed. Again, the husband is excused: he had committed incest in spite of himself.

There were two reasons why responsibility was put on to the man in this way. First, women were by nature passive, in particular in the acts of love. They were objects whom men, young and old, lay in wait for, bent to their will and played with. 'Have you spied on women in the bath, naked? Have you stroked women's breasts? Have you manipulated their shame?' It was to men that the questions were put. Women were sinners only when they stepped out of their role and procured their pleasure themselves, that is, when they acted like men. They sinned also when they, whom God had wanted to be tender, unarmed (*inermis*), placed under masculine protection, dared to devise their own weapons, that is potions, spells and charms; or when they defied male power, unreasonably (*irrationabiliter*), departing from the field of clearly ordained social relations, when they acted out of sight of their husbands in the area allocated to them in the innermost recesses of the house, where, amongst themselves, wives and maidservants looked after the young children, prepared the dead for their entry into the hereafter, dreamt of revenge and exchanged secrets and caresses. Second, and above all, the man was the master of the woman. He was responsible for the deeds and the thoughts of the woman he had married. It was his duty to forbid what he saw her do openly and what he heard her say openly that was displeasing to God. And if other women in the house, his daughters and his sisters, and even the slatterns in the kitchen, repeated in chorus the refrains that the Church condemned, it was his duty, rod in hand, to make them shut up. All the questions concerning spells, divination and conniving with demons, like those referring to the sexual practices that the priests forbade the couple to perform, were therefore put to men, and not to women, who were irresponsible.

For the man was their 'lord and master'. They were subject to him and there are, throughout the *Decretum*, frequent references to the conciliar texts to support this premise. I will note two. In Book XI, Burchard transcribed the words of the oath that the husband and his wife were required to swear when the bishop had reconciled them. The man says simply: 'I will keep her in future as a husband ought, according to the law, to keep his wife, cherishing her, and [my italics] *in the necessary discipline*; I will never leave her nor take another woman as long as she lives.' The woman spoke at greater length, since she promised more.

In future I will keep him and embrace him [this is the posture that the good wife should adopt, caressing, consoling and heartening, a supple Thetis at the feet of an imperious bronze

Jupiter] and I will be *subject* [my italics] to him, *obedient, in service* [should I translate this 'in servitude'?], in love and *in fear*, as according to the law the wife ought to be *subject* to the husband. I will never leave him and as long as he lives I will not bind myself to another man in marriage or in adultery.

On the part of the woman, we find servitude, trembling and shame, and on her part, and hers alone, adultery and the terrible penalties that punished it. The other text, Book VIII, repeats that women ought not to appear at public meetings to which they had not been summoned, and that certainly they had the right to speak and to discuss, but only among themselves, regarding their own womanly concerns, and in that part of the house from which they rarely emerged, and then always accompanied. But it is precisely here, in this retreat, that women acted, and not always correctly. The master of the house could not be held responsible for their failings. He rarely entered that obscure zone, where he was met with silence and where he saw nothing. God, however, saw everything. The priests, including the 'simplest', stood in for God and ought to see all. They were substitutes for the husband, the father and the brother. This is why forty-one specific questions were added to the first forty-eight. They revealed to the confessor where sin was concealed. They taught him the words capable of making it emerge. Lastly, since the *Corrector* is also a penitential, it lays down for each fault the level of fine that would satisfy God the Judge.

At this period, sin was redeemed by a corporal punishment that demonstrated the fault externally, by a way of behaving and of dressing. This punishment lasted a longer or shorter time according to the gravity of the fault. The scale of punishments seems to be based on the penalty inflicted on the murderer, that is, seven years. Both Regino and Burchard chose to copy out the decision of a council held at Tribur in 895 which described in minute detail the renunciations that the Church imposed on the guilty person.

First, he does not have the right to enter a church during the following forty days. Let him walk barefoot, without using a vehicle. Let him be dressed in woollen cloth and without shoes [it was a public murder, hence a male crime, and it is male dress that is at issue here] and without weapons. He will consume nothing during these forty days except bread, salt and pure water. He will neither eat nor drink in the company of other Christians or of other penitents until the forty days have elapsed, and no one will share his food. Depending on his status and his state of health, he may be permitted, out of mercy, to take fruit, herbs and vegetables, in particular if he has committed murder not of his own accord but from force. In any case, he is forbidden by canonical authority to have sex with any woman during these forty days, or to approach his wife, or to sleep with a man. Let him remain close to a church and, for his fault, be day and night before the door, let him not wander hither and thither but stay in one place. If he is threatened with death, the penance will be deferred until the bishop has restored peace between him and his enemies. If an illness afflicts him that prevents him from doing penance properly, it will be deferred until he is better. In the case of a long illness, the bishop will decide how to heal the sinner and the invalid. When the forty days are over, washed in running water [as, at the start of a new life, the body of the newborn baby and the body of a dead person were washed, and as, in the twelfth century, that of the future knight would be washed], he will resume his clothes and his shoes and will cut his hair. For the whole of the first year, after this fast, he will abstain from wine, mead, beer, meat, cheese and oily fish, except on feast days and except if he makes a long journey, rejoins the army or the court, or if he falls ill. In this case, he may compensate for the abstinence of Wednesdays, Fridays and Saturdays by giving each day a silver coin or by feeding three poor persons, and this until he returns home or is cured. At the end of this year, he will enter the church and he will be given the kiss of peace.

The same obligations continued during the second and third years. For the four following years, the sinner made only three fasts: before Easter, around St John's Day and before Christmas. 'At the end, he will receive holy communion.'

The punishments laid down for female sinners range very

widely, from three days to ten years of privations. The
penalty for having worked on Sunday, chattered in church
or neglected the sick was only a few days on bread and
water. For those who rendered an unfaithful lover impotent
or who diminished the excessive potency of a husband with
mixtures, it was a little longer, forty days, a *carina*. The
penalties punishing neglect of young children and the various
ways of casting spells and of taking pleasure with other
women were much heavier, ranging from one year (for
onanism) to five or six years (for using a phallic 'machine',
selling oneself or selling other women). Six sins were punished as severely as murder: poisoning, countering the judgement of God by talismans, teaching how to procure an
abortion, indulging in that most abject of sexual deviancies,
bestiality, drinking the sperm of one's husband and finally
that dream of going out at night into those strange countries
where they grilled the hearts of men. Lastly, abortion and
killing a man were punished beyond the seven-year marker.
Does this barometer accurately reflect the judgements passed
by priests at this period on the various degrees of female
guilt? It would be unwise to assume so. Burchard had not
constructed it himself. Respectful of the authorities, he
copied out, for each sin, the tariff imposed by earlier prescripts that came from every age and provenance, making a
few, but very few, alterations. Two facts, however, stand
out. First, we see the primordial desire to prevent women
from making attempts on life (but also, we should note, of
appropriating the seeds of this life, semen, the virile force at
its source); abusing one's body and practising magic were
judged less serious. More remarkable still, with regard to
'superstitions' and sexuality, is the blatant disparity between
the two sections of the questionnaire: in the case of women,
rigour, in the case of men, moderation and a surprising
laxity. For the man who believed in fairies or in omens, who
slept with a woman without affection, who used a 'machine'
to masturbate or who caressed another man, the penance
lasted only a few days. Whereas between three and five years
of public lamentations, of fasting and of very strict abstinence
were necessary to redeem the fault of lesbians or of those

crazy women who imagined themselves riding out at night in the company of she-devils.

This suggests that the code, constructed by men, was intended as a defensive weapon. Homosexual activity and the relations that women maintained with Diana and the Fates, those other women who helped them set their traps, and also those sorceresses who, like a lord leading his knights, led their vassals on fantastical rides, were fiercely condemned not only as an intolerable assertion of independence, but as an even more execrable inversion of the natural order, which reserved the active and dominant position in love to men. In so doing, was this repressive code not attacking everything that strengthened the cohesion of the enemy camp and the bases of its resistance to male domination? It aimed, furthermore, to dash from between the hands of women the instruments of their aggressions.

At this period, men were afraid of this mysterious, debilitating and deadly arsenal. The priests forbade them to believe in the virtue of brews and spells. But the priests believed in it themselves, and all men with them. If they felt their strength fail, it was, they were convinced, the effect of philtres, tisanes or those stimulants that drove men to make love too fiercely. Was it so very uncommon for a man, at night, at the moment of dropping off, to tremble at the idea that the apparently inoffensive wife who lay by his side might well, as he slept, take out his heart and put a handful of hay in its place? Husbands were therefore not hostile to their wife appearing alone before a judge other than themselves. She might perhaps speak more freely to him, and confess to depravities resolutely concealed. The woman questioned in this way was, in fact, triply disadvantaged: because the judge was a man, hence her natural superior; because this man was not her husband, and she could not wrap herself around him, soften him, sway or deceive him with soft assurances; and because he was a priest, and therefore insensible, in principle, as a result of his status, to her powers of seduction.

To ask women, at least the most noble of them, to confide in a man of the Church was to treat them like persons, capable of correcting themselves. But it was also to capture them. The Church got them in its clutches. On the threshold of the twelfth century, the period when Burchard of Worms was at work, an event of considerable importance took place in Europe. It changed the relations between men and women, and profoundly marked the whole of European culture, and its repercussions are still felt. The Church, by far the most important institution in existence, and growing in power as it purged its personnel and freed itself from all external influence, decided to bring sexuality under its strict control. It was at that time dominated by the monastic ethos. The majority of its rulers, and the most enterprising of them, were former monks, who saw themselves as angels. As such, they claimed to have no sex and prided themselves on their virginity, professing a horror of sexual stain. The Church, consequently, divided men into two groups. It forbade the servants of God to use their sexual organs; it allowed the rest to do so, but on the draconian conditions that it laid down. There remained women, dangerous, since everything revolved around them. The Church decided to subjugate them. To this end, it clearly defined the sins that women, by their constitutions, were inclined to commit. At the time that Burchard was drawing up the list of these specific faults, the ecclesiastical authorities were stepping up their efforts to regulate the institution of marriage. To impose a morality of marriage and to direct the consciences of women were one and the same project and the same battle. It was a long one. In the end, it transferred to priests the power of fathers to place the hand of their daughter in that of a son-in-law, and interposed a confessor between the husband and his wife.

Had the Church already grasped that the surest means of keeping its hold over men was to appropriate the ascendancy they exercised over the other sex? Had it appreciated the risk of provoking distrust and jealousy in men's minds, or hostility towards the intruder, and of giving rise to that profound anti-clericalism whose earliest manifestations are visible in the documents a century and a half later?

A hundred and seventy years later, the bishop of Rennes spoke in his turn. Obviously, he was in the husbands' camp.

Those powerful men, reputedly wise, who set an example and supervised the education of the younger boys, were the audience for whom the *Book of Manners* was primarily intended, and that is why the women whose weaknesses the sermon denounced were ladies and married. Stephen of Fougères was sure of winning round the heads of families if he laughed with them at secret female pleasures, and if he emphasized the dangers of trusting blindly in one's wife. In an effort to please them, therefore, he reread Burchard. He diverged from him very little, but adapted him. In Stephen's day, the husband was still afraid that he might be bewitched or unmanned by his wife, but he was just as fearful of her indocility and her moods, and he dreaded above all that she might deceive him. This explains a first difference between the *Book of Manners* and the *Decretum*. The latter referred to fornication and adultery only in the common question-naire, and it was the husband alone who was held respons-ible. At the end of the twelfth century, and this is surely one of the clearest aspects of any 'promotion' of women at this period, the wife was no longer regarded as passive in such affairs. She acted, and her motive was *amor*, the appetite for pleasure. In the meantime, high society had become familiar with the games of the love we call courtly. The success of this pleasurable activity is evident during the years when Stephen of Fougères was composing his diatribe. In verse 1059, the word 'jovente' (youth), the *joven* of the trouba-dours, came naturally to his pen immediately after the word 'love'. In this game, the convention was for the lover to be aroused by the sight of a beautiful woman. This led the lady to take pains with her appearance. Now responsible, she was guilty as soon as she got herself up to attract and make men look at her, employing all the finery that the courtly world, now much less crude, had adopted, such as precious fabrics and perfumes. The rather unsavoury mixtures that the *Med-icus* accused wives of using to arouse the ardour of their husband had been succeeded by cosmetics, ointments and all the artifices employed by women to show off their body and conceal its faults and the signs of age. Further, the man she was attempting to inflame was no longer the husband, but the lover. An active party, and therefore guilty, the lady was now at fault not only when she played 'against nature' with her women friends or her little boy, but when she went out in search of pleasure. In the *Book of Manners*, the truth of courtly love is revealed. The chosen lady is not simply the object of desire; she, too, desires. Far from pushing away the hands that were slipped under her mantle, she took the initiative; she, too, gave chase.

A further difference is that Stephen of Fougères shows white as well as black. In this, he is copying Marbode, who, in the *Book of Ten Chapters*, had followed chapter III, 'The prostitute', with a fourth chapter, 'The matron'. The apologia thus follows the indictment. It is much duller, obviously, as are descriptions of Paradise compared with those of Hell. Here again, the woman described is a lady and married. In fact, it was through marriage that the women of this period attained a social existence. Before it, they were nothing: the word *mesquine*, which came to mean something of small value, meant 'young girl' in the twelfth century. It was also marriage that, through the baseness of the wife, *amor*, ferment of disorder, destroyed. Lastly, it was within the context of marriage that morality taught how decently to use a female body. The conjugal cell was indeed the battlefield on which the two sexes waged war, but it was also the garden in which grew the virtues proper to the 'order of women', a sort of congregation resembling the orders of knights, priests and workers, over which the Church, in its conception of a balanced society, claimed to exercise control.

In the ritual of marriage, its gestures and formulas, the obligations of the woman are given clear expression. Stephen of Fougères lists them when celebrating the exemplary wife: she ought to love, serve and counsel the man to whom she had been given, loyally and without telling lies. These were exactly the duties of the vassal towards his lord. In exchange, like the vassal, the woman expected protection and assistance. Marriage, guarantee of the social order, subordinated women to robust male power. Submissive, prostrated and docile, the wife became the 'ornament' of her master.

She was also his delight. The word 'joy' occurs three times

in the poem. In the Romance language, joy corresponded to *gaudium*, the Latin term the clerks invariably used when they had to describe a marriage ceremony, because this word suggested the idea of the satisfaction one felt in sex. And this same word, 'joy', was spontaneously identified by those at the court of Henry Plantagenet, most of whom were multi-lingual, with the word *joi* in Occitanian love songs, also suggestive of sexual pleasure. There can be no doubt that the bishop of Rennes was referring to the pleasures of the body. Was this pleasure shared? One might, at first, conclude that it was. In verse 1173, the poem says: 'they were joyful', mutually. Six verses later, however, the brutal truth is revealed. Joy is what 'the husband has in the wife'. He alone is active, the master of ceremonies. Indeed, a little higher up, the prelate had roundly condemned the woman who dared to 'act the man'. At all events, the main point is that, according to Stephen, the first virtue of marriage was to justify male pleasure, to disassociate sexual pleasure from 'folly', to bring it out into the open, freed from guilt, in fact marriage as a cure for fornication. There was still, of course, some sin, but it was venial, 'without too heavy a penance'. Stephen of Fougères was shrewd; addressing the laity, he allowed for the joys of sex.

Yet, women could not attain perfection before they had been subdued, before their passions had subsided and their sons, whom they were too prone to coddle and smother with kisses, had passed the age of seven and put off their childish garments. This was the case with the countess of Hereford, whom the bishop sycophantically quoted as example. She had not yet entered the reassuring 'estate' of widowhood; she was on her third husband, but, like him, had seemingly much calmed down. Young men had ceased to speak to her of *amor*. Respectful and impervious, they 'honoured her greatly'. Cecily was the model of the great lady in decline. Women such as she now found all their enjoyment in God alone, and served 'God's poor', that is the men of prayer, employing for their benefit that admirable feminine manual dexterity that Dudo of Saint-Quentin had praised in the mistresses of the dukes of Normandy, but here devoted to highly respectable tasks, applied to the pieces of embroidery that, when they were young, women neglected in their folly. The sermon thus ends with a eulogy of old age, which finally delivered women from their demons.

The husbands who listened to Stephen of Fougères all dreamed of the perfect wife. Admittedly, they would have liked her not to be too composed when in their bed. But they knew what to expect, convinced that women were insufferable and harmful, and that, perfidiously, they slipped through one's fingers until old age deprived them of their femininity and made them into a sort of slightly less rugged man. The tragedy was that, at the same time, they ceased to look attractive. Did you prefer them spirited or safe? It was a difficult choice. There remained the immemorial fear and anxiety. In the *Book of Manners*, in the *Decretum* of Burchard of Worms before it, and earlier in the questionnaire of Regino of Prüm and in so many other even older writings, over the centuries, we find the same old refrain: women were in league with the devil, they were cantankerous and impossible, their bodies, like that of the chimera, were unquenchable infernos. The curse went back a long way, to the creation of the world. Which knight had never, at one time or another, recognized in the wife lying beside him the features of the woman whose image was everywhere on display, associated with death, perdition and that sin which was for him the worst, perhaps the only, at any rate the only one of which he was persuaded by the reactions of his body, the sin of the flesh? Which of them had never, at some time, recognized Eve?

2

The Fall

E ve is the heroine of a story told everywhere, in words and pictures, in the twelfth century. The story appears in the Bible, at the beginning of the book of Genesis. It tells of the origins of the human race, the foundation of the moral and social order and, in a few sentences, gives a global explanation of the human condition. This very simple explanation was endlessly repeated and universally accepted. It provided answers to three questions: why was humanity sexual, why was it guilty and why was it unhappy?

In fact, there are two stories in the opening pages of Genesis. In the first, God said: 'Let us make man in our image, after our likeness ... Male and female created He them. And God blessed them, and said unto them, Be fruitful and multiply, and replenish the earth, and subdue it.' The second story is more detailed: God 'formed man of the dust of the ground and breathed into his nostrils the breath of life'. He put him in a garden He had planted, to cultivate and watch over it, authorizing him to eat 'of every tree in the garden' except, under pain of death, 'of the tree of the knowledge of good and evil'. God then said: 'It is not good that the man should be alone; I will make him an helpmeet for him.' Next, He 'formed every beast of the field and every fowl of the air' and 'brought them unto Adam to see what he would call them'. But 'for Adam there was not found an

helpmeet'. Then God 'caused a deep sleep to fall on Adam
... and He took one of his ribs, and closed up the flesh
instead thereof. And the rib, which the Lord God had taken
from man, made He a woman, and brought her unto the
man. And Adam said, This is now bone of my bones, and
flesh of my flesh; she shall be called woman because she was
taken out of man. Therefore shall a man leave his father and
his mother and shall cleave unto his wife and they shall be
one flesh.' They were both naked and 'were not ashamed'.
We, however, feel shame. Why is this? The next part of the
story answers this second question.

A serpent spoke to the woman. The dialogue begins with
the serpent asking why they do not eat of every tree in the
garden. Eve replies: 'The fruit of the tree which is in the
midst of the garden, God hath said, Ye shall not eat of it ...
lest ye die.' The serpent then says: 'Ye shall surely not die:
For God doth know that in the day ye eat thereof, then your
eyes shall be opened, and ye shall be as gods, knowing good
and evil.' The woman saw that the tree 'was good for food,
and that it was pleasant to the eyes ... she took of the fruit
thereof, and did eat, and gave also unto her husband with
her; and he did eat ... and the eyes of both of them were
opened, and they knew that they were naked.' They made
themselves loincloths of fig leaves, and when they heard God
approaching, they hid. God said to the man: 'Who told thee
that thou wast naked? Hast thou eaten of the tree?'

The answer to the third question follows. God questioned
them, beginning with Adam, who replied: 'The woman
whom Thou gavest to be with me, she gave me of the tree,
and I did eat.' The woman then says: 'The serpent beguiled
me, and I did eat.' God judged and condemned, first the
serpent, then the woman, to whom He said: 'I will greatly
multiply thy sorrow and thy conception; in sorrow thou shalt
bring forth children; and thy desire shall be to thy husband,
and he shall rule over thee.' Adam is then condemned. It is
at this point that he names his wife, as he had previously
named the animals; he gives her the name Eve, 'because she
was the mother of all living'. Seeing that 'the man is become
as one of us', fearing that he will eat also of the tree of life

'and live for ever', God expels him from the garden of Eden. It was only then that 'Adam knew Eve his wife; and she conceived, and bore Cain'.

In the twelfth century, within the monasteries and around the cathedrals, men of the Church sought to deepen their understanding of this text. They scrutinized the meaning of each word for the benefit of those whose job it was to spread the message among the people. I will discuss five of these commentaries, works by Robert (or Rupert) of Liège (or of Deutz) and by Abelard, and then those of Peter Comestor and of Hugh and Andrew of Saint-Victor, all three of whom were active in Paris at a slightly later date. These scholars did not, of course, start from scratch. They based themselves on precursors whose works they drew on and added to. I will also discuss, therefore, the 'authorities' to whom they referred, the Venerable Bede (beginning of the eighth century), Alcuin (end of the eighth century), Rabanus Maurus (ninth century) and, lastly, the master of them all, St Augustine. I will show how, during the course of the three acts of the drama – the Creation, the Temptation and the Punishment – the figure of Eve is illumined by the reflections of these Doctors.

The most profound of the commentaries on Genesis was written by St Augustine in answer to the Manichaeans. It consists of a series of metaphors that are based on two sentences in the story. The first was *masculum et feminam fecit eos* (male and female created he them), which for Augustine meant that there was male and female in each human being. The second was *facimus ei adjutorium similis ejus* (I will make him an helpmeet for him); the woman was in the likeness of the man, but she was, nevertheless, his helpmeet, which presupposed that she was subject to him, like the worker to the foreman. In fact, the whole created world was constructed on a hierarchical framework; one directed – here it was the man – the other 'complied' – in this case the woman. These two axioms of the founding myth reveal the nature of man and uphold the morality that ought to govern the human race. Man is made of a carnal part, the body, and a spiritual part, the soul, the former subject to the latter. Within the soul, and in the same hierarchical relationship, there coexist the *pars animalis*, by which the body is ruled, and *ratio*, to which the 'animal part' is subordinate. *Ratio* is described as *virilis*: reason is simply the masculine principal; the feminine is identified with *appetitus*, that is, desire. Women, like men, are endowed with reason, but the animal part, that which desires, is predominant in women, whereas in men, it is the reasonable, hence the spiritual, that prevails. The man, consequently, dominates, an intermediary between God, source of wisdom, whom he should obey, and woman, over whom he should rule. This is what Adam discovered when he emerged from the deep sleep into which he had been plunged by God: the woman had come from him, hence was in substance similar to him, but she was only a tiny part of him, so naturally subject to him.

We find few traces of this magisterial interpretation in the glosses of the twelfth century, except in Robert of Liège, who says: 'Except by sex, the *substantia* of women is no different from that of men, although, by the dignity of their condition, they are less superior than men to the animals, but they are not less rational and they aspire no less to resemble their Creator.' The other masters who pondered this Scriptural passage referred to the second commentary of St Augustine. This was *ad litteram*, drawing out from the text its first, immediate and literal meaning, word for word, as they did themselves when they read in front of their disciples. The most important of their observations are linked to five of the Latin words in the Vulgate: *adjutorium* (helpmeet), *sopor* (sleep), *edificavit* (he built, with the rib), *relinquet* (he shall leave) and *nudi* (they were naked).

With regard to the word *adjutorium*, they added nothing to the propositions of St Augustine. In what, he had said, did Adam have need of a helpmeet? The woman could serve no purpose except to make children, 'as the earth is a helper to the seed' (the image of a woman open like a ploughed field to a man, who alone was active, embedding the seed, immediately springing to his mind). What else was she for? Was she to cultivate the garden of Eden? A second strong

man would have been of more use. Was she to comfort
Adam in his solitude? No, since the bishop of Hippo did not
doubt – nor did the men of the twelfth century doubt – that
when it came to conversation, or living together, two friends
got on a good deal better than a husband and wife, whose
wishes were contradictory, given that the former ought to
rule and the latter was usually reluctant to obey. So, if it had
not been a man that God took from Adam's side, it was
because He wanted the human race to be fruitful and
multiply. The sole reason why the woman was 'created as an
helpmeet' was, therefore, procreation. This being so, continued St Augustine, why were there no 'honourable unions
in an immaculate bed' in Paradise? There was nothing to
prevent children of the seed of Adam and Eve being born
'without the troublesome ardour of desire and without the
pains of childbirth'. They had simply not had enough time to
sleep together. 'Hardly had they been created when the
transgression took place, as a result of the woman.'

Augustine saw *sopor* as a moment of ecstasy during which
Adam was transported to join the 'court of angels, and from
which he returned announcing like a prophet the great sign'.
Magnum sacramentum. The mystery of grace, said Bede.
Adam prefigured Christ, in a torpor, in His agony on the
Cross, while from His side ran the water and the blood from
which the Church was created. Whereas Rabanus Maurus
emphasized the contemplation that one could only fully
attain by a withdrawal into the secrecy of silence, and that –
we catch here a faint echo of the *Contra manicheos* – allows
one to discover in oneself 'what ought to govern, like the
man, what ought to be governed, like the woman'.

St Augustine passed quickly over *edificavit*. With the rib,
he said, God had made Eve 'like a house'. In connection with
this construction, however, the commentary was expanded
in the twelfth century, which is hardly surprising, given that
a theology and a morality of marriage were then being
developed. Why, asked Robert, did God not make the
woman from the dust of the earth? Why did he use a piece
of the man's body, if not to show that *caritas*, the bond of
the monogamous union, ought to be indissoluble? 'If the

man separates from his wife for any reason, except fornication, lacking a rib, he is no longer complete.' For the woman, it was far worse. 'If she abandons her husband, she will no longer matter to God, because she is not, to begin with, a complete body or a complete flesh, but only a part taken from a man.' Whereas for Hugh of Saint-Victor, if the woman was made from a rib, and not from the head or the feet, it was because she ought to be neither dominant nor subservient, but a partner.

Both Hugh and Andrew also emphasized Adam's 'prophesy' (a man shall leave his father and his mother), that is, the word *reliquet*, which their predecessors had hardly discussed. This word, said Hugh, meant that a man ought not to join carnally with someone of his family, but also that, in marrying, he freed himself from paternal tutelage in order to manage his own family, transferring to his wife the *dilectio*, the special affection, a son owed his progenitors. Andrew went further. He spoke not of *dilectio* but of love, though specifying that this love was 'spiritual, and stronger than the carnal love by which the couple cherish each other mutually'. We observe the idea of love as a normal element within the conjugal couple emerging in the last decades of the twelfth century. This was a pure love, obviously, transcending the appetites of the flesh, sublimating and tending to justify them. The verb *amare* was therefore not enough; it needed *adamare*, which strengthened it, to express a 'vehemence' by which the two fleshes were made one. Here, Andrew repeated the arguments of his master, saying that 'the *dilectio* between a man and a woman ought to be so strong that the mind of each made no distinction between the flesh it invigorated and the beloved flesh of the spouse that it longed to inhabit, each the other, if such a thing were possible.' It was not, but at least the two 'minds' merged in the procreation of a single flesh.

Because scholarly attention was at this time focused on sin as well as on the marriage contract, and because the sacrament of penance was being perfected at the same time as the sacrament of marriage, the commentary on the word *nudi* was expanded on in the twelfth century. St Augustine had, of course, discussed this word, deducing from it that, in Paradise, the 'animal body' did not have the 'desire for carnal pleasure'. Citing St Paul's Epistle to the Romans ('I see another law in my members, warring against the law of my mind, and bringing me into captivity to the law of sin which is in my members'), he had said: 'Why should we not believe that, before sin, man had been able, in order to procreate sons, to command his genital members like the others that his soul prompts for such-and-such a task, without turmoil and without an irrepressible urge for sensual pleasure?' Man had disobeyed, so he had deserved to have placed in his body the impulse of that law that contradicted the law of the mind, an impulse on which 'marriage imposed order and which continence restrained'. Robert, Andrew of Saint-Victor and Peter Comestor all returned to this point. Andrew thought that the 'shameful parts' were very well named because of their 'illicit and bestial impulse which proceeds from sin'. For Robert, this urge revealed both the weakness of the flesh and its natural rebellion against the mind. It was 'disorderly' and 'shameful', said Peter, 'because it does not happen without sin'. This was true even in marriage; admittedly, there was an 'excuse' for the sin, but the 'shame' remained, and that concern of the spouses not to be seen, and not to make love in public.

So, in the twelfth century, learned men found in Adam's 'prophesy' the justification for the effort being put by the Church into controlling sexuality and into imposing order on the *inordinatio* of the flesh, and this in the context of marriage. For them, consequently, the woman of the Scriptures was primarily the wife. In the school of Saint-Victor, their scholarly reflections led them to see the female condition as a little less base. Because she was taken from the side of a man, woman was constructed on the same model as he; she was therefore a rational being; and this similarity of structure rendered spiritual love capable of fully realizing the union of two fleshes. Further, the 'partner', companion and wife had a right over the body of her husband by virtue of a necessary mutual affection, which, towards the end of the century, tended to resemble pure love, the *fin'amor* extolled in the courtly literature.

Nevertheless, the text of Genesis also further strengthened the rock-solid conviction that the woman, the helpmeet, had been put alongside the man only in order to be 'known', to become a wife and above all a mother, a receptacle, a womb primed for the germination of the male seed, and that she had no other function than to be impregnated, and that had it not been for this role the world could quite easily have managed without her. Lastly, the story of the Creation confirmed in the masters who trained the preachers their conviction that the burden of sensuality, that is, of sin, of that 'animal part' that should be controlled by reason, weighed more heavily on women, that reason was predominant in men, and that this predominance conferred on men *imperium* over women.

The scene of the temptation and its three characters, the serpent, the woman and the man, lay at the heart of the myth, and it is this scene that was most often represented in pictures, in drama and in speech. St Augustine, however, said little about it. The woman, he emphasized, disobeyed knowingly, aware of the facts; she did not have the excuse of having forgotten God's commandment; was it not she who had first mentioned it in the dialogue with the tempter? What led her to defy the edict? It was first desire, the *amor proprie potestatis*, the love of – that is to say, the desire for – an autonomous power, and then 'prideful self-presumption': the sin, said the master, was dictated by pride. In the commentary against the Manichaeans, the drama is transposed to the interior of the soul. When we sin, the serpent takes the role of 'suggestion', that proposition which, coming from the brain or from sensory perception, from sight, touch or from all the senses, incites to sin; woman is greed, that impulse in us to seize what tempts us; man, lastly, is reason. If reason resists 'in a virile manner', we are saved. 'If it consents, if it decides to do that which desire urges, we are expelled from Paradise.' Pride, greed and desire are all present, but we should note that, at the beginning of the fifth century, the bishop of Hippo did not explicitly implicate carnal lust.

Three centuries later, in a monastery, the change has

begun. The serpent, said the Venerable Bede, deceived the woman, not the man, 'because our reason cannot be silenced if there is no pleasure and *carnal pleasure* [my italics]'. *Cupiditas* has become *delectatio carnalis*, sexual pleasure, denounced as both female and culpable. Sin operated in three stages: 'The serpent advises pleasure, the sensuality of the animal body [the feminine in us] obeys, and reason consents.' And it is the woman who picked the apple and offered it to the man 'because, after the pleasure of *carnal* [my italics] desire, reason is driven to sin'. Rabanus Maurus follows suit, citing Gregory the Great ('Eve, like the flesh, submits to pleasure. Adam, like the mind, consents, conquered by suggestion and pleasure'). He emphasizes sight: Eve would never have touched the tree if she had not first unwisely looked at it; 'she went to her death by the eyes'; let us beware, let us protect ourselves from the sight of forbidden things. Did this mean women? Rabanus, like Bede a monk, clearly accentuates the sexual. Eve was certainly tempted by vain glory, by the greed that is a taste not only for amassing money, but for seizing every opportunity to raise oneself up. But she succumbed above all to the appetite for sexual pleasure. Once again, it is in the choice of words that the new interpretation is expressed. To what did Adam's mind succumb? To seductions: *illecebrae*. There are many different sorts, of course, but it is clear that this Latin word evoked first the appeals of sex. What is it that incites us to sin? 'Lubricious thoughts.' Let us be wary of 'lascivious desires'. In the monastic world of the ninth century, it was generally accepted that the sin was the woman and the forbidden fruit was sex.

Of the twelfth-century glossators, Hugh of Saint-Victor is the only one to repeat Rabanus Maurus. The others, meditating on the responsibility of the sinner, followed St Augustine. Thus, for Robert, God had made man right, *rectus*. What is rectitude? It is when the superior mind directs the flesh, when the rational mind mediates between God and the flesh, obeying God and commanding the flesh. Sin is thus a subversion of the natural order, the spiritual debasing itself to submit to the carnal. And Robert here reflected on the role of the woman. It was not so much that she was sensual but that she was *vaga*, unstable, inconstant, 'straying in the body and the eyes', wandering across the beautiful garden, looking around her, full of curiosity. She heard a serpent speak. How could anyone believe that a serpent could speak? In fact, Eve thought that through it there spoke a spirit that she took for divine. She was duped, as so many women are who allow themselves to be taken in by fallacious speeches. In fact, women were frivolous. They were also deceitful. When she replied to the serpent, Eve distorted God's commandment, referring not to the tree of knowledge but to that 'which is in the midst of the garden'. Finally, 'giving the fruit to her man', she did not seduce him strictly speaking, nor did she seek to make him believe what she had herself believed. Not a word was spoken. With a gesture, she commanded, *imperando*; she was imperious, like all women. She compelled the man to obey her voice rather than that of God. This was the abuse, *imperium abusivum*, *importunitas* of the female, what was intolerable. This desire to command was Eve's second sin. For she had doubly sinned, against God and against man. Hence she was doubly punished, not only, like Adam, by physical pain, but by her subjection to male power. This was why, since the Fall, women ought to hide not only their sex, as men do, but their heads, proclaiming the shame both of the ardours of their womb and their 'imperious temerity'. In this commentary, the reading of Genesis develops into an indictment of the failings of the female nature, those vices whose victims were men. The charge reappears in Andrew of Saint-Victor, but toned down: the serpent addressed the woman because it believed her to be 'simpler', less wily, to the point of believing that a serpent could speak. But it returned, just as violently, in Peter Comestor.

Abelard went much further than the others. Man is the image of God, woman is only a semblance. Man, closer to God, is thus more perfect; he has lordship over women as over all other creatures; his wisdom gives him greater dignity; he is also more affectionate, from the love he feels for the woman it is his task to direct. As a result, it was not him, first, that the serpent set out to seduce. And second, if he took the apple offered to him by his wife, it was from love of her, so as not to 'sadden' her (this came from St Augustine, who said: 'Adam did not wish to sadden her, believing that she would pine away without his affection, if she felt herself detached from his spirit') and because he presumed too much on divine mercy; the offence seemed to him slight, especially since it had been committed less from malice than from affection. Third, 'Who would disagree that God had been more fully loved by him than by the woman?'; she did not love God, since she could believe that He spoke to her through the serpent and that He tricked her.

In the twelfth century, Christianity was no longer so much a matter of rites and observances as of conduct and morality. The spread of the practices of private penitence gave greater urgency to the questions: what is sin? where is it? In women more than in men, replied the scholars: read the Bible. Adam was not seduced, he did not talk nonsense. He was too loving towards his partner and he avoided hurting her. Whereas Eve was no longer accused of pride, but of the second of the evil tendencies detected by St Augustine, the desire to prevail over the man, against the provisions of the Creator, and most of all of fickleness, stupidity and, finally, sensuality. That Eve had been above all moulded by libidinous greed was a fact so generally accepted that, with the exception of Hugh, twelfth-century commentators did not feel it necessary to labour the point. The Fall, they had no doubt, was provoked by the appetite for pleasure.

Thus they reversed the relationship between sexuality and sin that had been established by St Augustine. He had shown the former as not the cause but the consequence of the latter. Once fallen, 'the body of the man took on that morbid and deadly quality which appears in the flesh of cattle, and that impulse seized him that impels cattle to copulate so that deaths will be followed by births.' The reasonable soul then began to feel shame at those impulses which perturbed the members of the flesh. It discovered modesty. The masters of the twelfth century remembered the words of the bishop of Hippo. But, like Robert, they did so to deplore the fact that

so few people regarded these 'involuntary impulses' which
make the genital organs constrict as the expression of the
'wrath of God' and for the punishment of the libido, and
that so few decided to 'sleep together with intent to procreate'. 'One sole cause motivates almost all of them, it is the
eagerness to satisfy a desire, and it eclipses not only respect for
God, but the conscience to engender.' Hugh of Saint-Victor,
too, thought that to burn with desire was a punishment, and
Peter Comestor described the explosion of sexuality after sin
in this way: 'The movements of concupiscence were natural,
but repressed and contained, as they are among children
before puberty, and they opened, like rivers and began to
move and to flow . . .'

Eve was punished by God. In the *Contra manicheos*, St
Augustine suggested reading the sentence 'spiritually not
carnally'. 'In sorrow thou shalt bring forth children': the
children, he explained, are good works, and the sorrow is
the effort to refrain from that to which the 'desire of the
flesh' inclines. His successors preferred to follow him in his
literal commentary, where, emphasizing the pride of Adam,
who, questioned by God, hid, and lacked the 'humility' to
confess his offence, he judged the male and the female equally
guilty, 'unequal in sex but equal in pride', hence together in
condemnation. However, for Eve the penalty was twofold:
her punishment was on the one hand to give birth, to prolong
life in pain, because, through her offence, death had entered
bodies, and on the other to be subject to the man. 'We should
not believe', said Augustine, 'that before sin the woman had
not been made to be dominated by the man, to "turn towards
him" and to serve him. But the "service" was of a different
kind, not that of the slave but that which, according to St
Paul, Christians rendered each other "out of love".' Before
sin, the submission was from 'love', after, it was of 'condition', of status. The woman was subjected to the domination that she was forbidden by St Paul from seeking to
exercise over her husband. By his verdict, the Creator she
had offended had thus humbled Eve and all her daughters.
'It is not nature but sin that made women deserve to have in

their husband a master, and if he is not served, nature is further corrupted and the sin aggravated.'

We find the same arguments almost word for word in Bede, Alcuin and Rabanus Maurus: woman, said the latter, 'under the power of the husband, serves God in fear; she rejoices in [her husband] not in tranquillity but in trembling; had she not sinned, she would have joined herself to him in the holy embraces of affection; but he must control her, master her carnal impulses and drag her [as Abelard dragged Héloïse] towards the redemption of the heavenly life.' Had she not deviated from discipline, she would have reigned with him, a 'partner', in 'liberty'.

In the twelfth century, the gloss on the third episode in the story was meagre, except in the case of Robert of Liège, who commented as a jurist. Before his judge, Adam pleaded not guilty, and his defence was not only *excusatio* but accusation. From the shelter of the trees, he attacked, he took issue with God, impudently, shifting the fault back on to Him, reproaching Him for having landed him with Eve, who harried him. As for her, she was equally presumptuous, evasive, answering one thing by another. For her, the punishment was threefold, 'three lashes of the whip on the female sex . . . because the quantity of the sin is three times greater in the woman than in the man': she had let herself be seduced, she had sought pleasure and she had made Adam share it. Hence, if death was the common punishment, God took 'special vengeance' on the woman. Because she had believed that she could become 'like the gods' and because God was the God of the living, she had deserved to be the mother of the dead; everything that she conceived in sin was destined to succumb, body and soul, if not given life by Christ. Bodily pain was the punishment for bodily pleasure, 'in her womb'. There was no hesitation as to the nature of the pleasures that the priests of this period condemned. Lastly, for that 'importunity' of women who hounded their husbands, the penalty was servitude. This is how Robert explained the words 'he shall rule over thee'. The word 'rule' is stronger than the word 'power'. The ascendancy of the husband over the wife was greater, consequently, than that of the father over his daughter. Thus, when they married, women saw their condition deteriorate. But, he added, the penalty is non-existent or very light for women who are 'chaste and faithful'. These words reveal once again the shift towards the sexual: what must be controlled in women, and strictly, was the inclination to debauchery and the propensity to adultery.

When God said: 'I will greatly multiply thy sorrow', the *multiplicatio* was not, as it was in the first story of the Creation ('be fruitful and multiply'), a blessing, but a punishment. 'In fact, the more fertile she is, the more a woman suffers. After each conception comes childbirth, hence pain. Her very blood torments her. In good health, she is plagued by her periods, she is the only animal to have them.' The wrath of God brings about 'the birth of all those men without whom the world would be a better place', who are conceived by chance, involuntarily, in the blind passion of lust. 'From pride of the spirit proceeds incontinence of the flesh, and from incontinence of the flesh the multiplication of conceptions.' All women, even the saintliest, with the exception of the Mother of God, conceived and conceive 'in iniquity', in filth and in sin, not only original sin but that incited by their own desire for sexual pleasure, which is simply a consequence of the first. For Adam and Eve engaged often in 'casual sex', not in the hope of producing descendants, but to quench the guilty ardour that devoured them.

Hugh of Saint-Victor's contribution is short but significant. For him, as for Peter Comestor, the punishment could not lie in the multiplication of conceptions. Did one not read in Exodus: 'the evil one is sterility'? Women were punished by the sufferings of childbirth, at the completion of pregnancies that frequent miscarriages and the cruelty of infant mortality rendered 'useless', and by that death of the soul which follows pleasure in all of us. Andrew agrees. He held that to get a woman pregnant was a 'happiness'. Did one suffer in conceiving? 'On the contrary, one enjoyed it, very much.'

This, then, was how the most learned priests of the twelfth century responded in the face of Eve and her troubles. She was undeniably inferior to Adam. This had been decided by God. He created man in His image, and woman from a tiny part of the man's body, as his imprint, or rather his reflection. Woman was never more than a reflection of an image of God. A reflection, as everybody knows, does not act independently. Only the man was in a position to act. The woman was passive, her movements dictated by those of her companion. This was the primordial order. Eve shattered it by bending Adam to her will. But God intervened, returned her to her place and increased her subjection to the man in punishment for her sin.

On this certainty, others were erected, substantiated by readings of the biblical texts. They gave support to the efforts of the priests to rescue society from evil. Since it was men who ruled and who acted, the reformers were concerned first to help them. They were now divided into two distinct categories, men of prayer, who were asexual, and the rest, who were sexual. The former, who included the commentators on Genesis, had to struggle to honour the rule of continence that was imposed on them. So we should not be surprised to see Peter Comestor, Robert or Hugh of Saint-Victor worrying about the 'disorderly movements' that they themselves had difficulty in mastering in certain of their limbs. Nor should we be surprised that, with the exception of Robert, who followed Rabanus Maurus and Gregory the Great, they did not adopt the Augustinian interpretation of the first story of the Creation, Augustine's way of transcending the myth of sexualization, seeing it as an illustration of the conflictual division within every human being between the rational and the *animalis*, between 'spirit' and 'lechery', and asserting that, coming from the devil, temptation triumphed with the assistance of 'that part which, in the unique man, is in the image of and on the model (*exemplum*) of the woman'. For them, at the source of every contravention of divine law was sex. The capital sin was that of the flesh. Inevitably, they saw in the drama played out beneath the trees of the Garden of Eden the irruption of the desire which tormented them. They identified with Adam, to whom Eve offered the apple. The forbidden fruit was the body of this woman, soft, lovely to look at, delectable. They knew what it was to be tempted and they felt very sympathetic towards Adam. They tended to play down the culpability of the man, and in so doing, their own. How were men to resist, surrounded by so many available women? That, for the priests of this period, women were objects delivered without resistance to masculine appetites, an apple munched in passing, is illustrated by a curious story told by the English chronicler Ralph of Coggeshall. Sometime around 1180, he says, Gervase of Tilbury, a canon, then a guest of the archbishop of Reims, was walking through the vineyards of Champagne. He came upon a young girl, found her to his taste, spoke to her 'courteously of lustful love', and made ready to go further. She rebuffed him and refused: 'If I lose my virginity, I shall be damned.' Gervase was flabbergasted; how could anyone resist him? It was obvious that this woman was not normal. She must be a heretic, one of those Cathars who clung stubbornly to the belief that all copulation was diabolical. He tried to reason with her, but in vain, so he denounced her. She was arrested and tried. The proof was incontrovertible and she was burned.

The men who were most vulnerable in the eyes of the scholars discussed here were those who were celibate – the clergy, their colleagues, and the unmarried knights. There were three places where women were poised, ready to corrupt them, three dangerous places where the hero must demonstrate his courage. The first was the town, and the red-light districts frequented by professionals, women who Hugh, Andrew and Peter Comestor, like their colleague, Peter the Chanter of Notre-Dame in Paris, believed did a job, a 'trade', and performed a necessary, even salutary, service, since there was need of them for all those men who burned. To buy their services to relieve themselves was, they decreed, a minor sin. They posed little threat to men of good society, who affected to disdain them. It was out in the country that men such as these were tempted, when, out riding, like Gervase of Tilbury, they came across shepherdesses. They seized hold of them and made them 'yield', as it said in the songs that were called pastorales. Consenting and ravished, in both senses of the word:

> I committed a folly
> became his love,
> but I really wanted to.

More often, however, the tempting fruit was offered inside the house, the vast noble house, teeming with women who were 'unclaimed' and available, whom it was hardly culpable to take, as adultery was not involved. Taking such women and masturbation were rated alike in the penitentials. For the young men, the danger came from the maidservants. For their elders, it came from those young girls whom, if we are to believe the romances, the laws of hospitality required should be placed at the disposal of itinerant knights. Or, and this was serious, the danger came from the mistress of the house. It is common, in the lives of saints, for the adolescent hero to be shown as obliged to resist the attacks of excited matrons. One of the biographies of St Bernard presents him, at the time when he was studying with the canons of Châtillon-sur-Seine, attacked one night in his bed by a naked girl; she slipped into the bed, remained still a moment, waiting, then took action, 'felt him, aroused him', without success, of course. A little later, in a castle where he was a guest, it was the lady who approached him. He defended himself, a new Joseph, but finally to get rid of her he had to cry out, waking the household. Such are the Eves we encounter everywhere we go!

The surest form of defence was to take one of them and establish her permanently in one's bed. Marriage was the best response. In the twelfth century, the Church authorities put the finishing touches to the structure of marriage, including it among the sacraments, the seventh. This had been a delicate operation, because the conjugal union was carnal, hence sinful, if only a little. How could it transmit grace? The intellectuals found their justification in Genesis. Marriage was instituted in Paradise by God the Father Himself, and was the only one of the sacraments to be distinguished in this way. They also found in the sacred text a basis for the principle of indissolubility, and justification for the prohibition of incest and the claim that only procreation exonerated from the pleasures of sex. The Scriptures taught, lastly, that within the couple, the woman was the fomenter of discord. If she had the upper hand, everything was turned upside down and went awry. Scripture itself, consequently, laid down that the lady ought to serve her lord and adopt before him a posture of humility, and asserted that it was not enough to 'govern' her, but that she must be subjugated; Peter Comestor saw the brutalities of defloration as the seal, the mark cruelly imprinted on the flesh, of this necessary enslavement. Andrew, admittedly, spoke also of love. But the overriding impression is nevertheless one of a *dominatio*, of an implacable 'lordship', and of an 'empire' of the husband.

In the last analysis, the priests used the words of Eve, her actions and the sentence that condemned her as an excuse to load the burden of sin on to women in order to disburden men. This inevitably led them vigorously to denounce the errors of women. They need only cast an eye over court society to recognize in the behaviour of wives the three faults committed by Adam's 'partner' beneath the boughs of the apple tree, which had caused the Fall. Like Eve, these women were in league with the devil. Like Eve, they were eaten up by the desire to make men submit to them. Like Eve, they were carried away by their taste for sexual pleasure. And we should remember that sorcery, aggression and lust were the three vices attacked by Stephen of Fougères.

These were the vices that, from the end of the eleventh century, the increasing number of men of prayer were striving to root out from the female soul, primarily in order to render women less harmful, to defuse them, and protect men better. In 1100, at the time when the features of the repentant sinner in the person of Mary Magdalen were overshadowing those of Mary, generous disciple and the friend of Jesus, and when the stories of Mary the Egyptian and other penitent courtesans, prostrated in salutary mortifications, were growing in popularity, men such as Robert of Arbrissel, Abelard and William Firmat were gathering around them wives who had been disappointed in marriage and daughters who refused it, and were, as a result, called whores; they consoled them and, to prevent them from doing harm, put them away in monasteries. Later, men of the Church tried to bring before the tribunal of penance the wives of great men, beginning with the most respectable, those 'holy women' evoked by Robert of Liège, who had remained in the world and led there an edifying life of piety. Would they be capable, in dialogue with the confessor, of exploring lucidly their conscience and of distinguishing good from evil? Yes, said the Bible, because there existed between the sexes no difference of 'substance', and because women, too, were rational beings. The story of the Creation thus contained the seeds of a spiritual promotion of women. Indeed, the most recent of the glossators I am discussing here, Andrew of Saint-Victor, went so far as to speak of equality between the female and the male as a possibility for the future, when sin would have been altogether driven out. Another reason why the beginning of Genesis was scrutinized so assiduously, was in order to give support to all those apostles who were striving to help virgins to remain pure, widows to remain chaste and ladies properly to perform their role as wives. They helped them by their words.

3

Speaking to Women

In the fourteenth and fifteenth centuries, the Church addressed itself to the masses. It spoke to them loudly and clearly, in the main squares of towns, in the surrounding fields and in the new churches whose plain and luminous architecture was expressly designed to allow the congregation to see the preacher and hear his words. Famous stars toured Europe, and news of their imminent arrival caused a stir in a city. Impatiently awaited, their sermons shook people up, triggering sudden outbursts of collective penance; worldly finery was burned, people lashed themselves; echoes of imprecations hurled against the devil and against sinners, and of moral laws decreed, lingered in the memory, and it was by this means that the ordinary people of Western Europe gradually became Christians. It would not be going too far to liken the upheaval in consciousness caused by the rise of preaching to the impact of the media today. In fact, this rise had started much earlier, at the turn of the eleventh and twelfth centuries, when the best priests had decided to live as the first disciples of Jesus had lived, hence to spread the good news, as they had done, across the world. They no longer confined themselves to performing the liturgical rites before the faithful, but set out to speak in a language they could understand, exhorting them to behave better and to follow the teaching of the Gospels. More than a century passed, however, before this mode of teaching was systematically organized in the dioceses. It took time to form reliable teams and to develop ways of holding the attention of the masses, and also for a context ripe for the diffusion of this message to be solidly established, that is, the town. It was at the very end of the twelfth century that, in northern France, the town effectively overtook the countryside, and it was at just this time that there appeared the oldest writings transmitting model sermons.

We are able, however, to read some of the words that churchmen were addressing to women long before. They are found in the letters written for them, letters which were preserved because they were little literary monuments. Their authors had chosen their Latin words with immense care, and arranged them according to the strict rules of rhetoric, positioning them in such a way that their cadences would impose on the text the solemn rhythms of high-flown eloquence. Letters of this sort were not written to reveal confidences, or to be read by their recipient in privacy and silence. They were intended to be declaimed before the assembled household, read in other houses, and news of them was meant gradually to be spread about. These were public words and these letters were copied. Brought together in collections, they took their place alongside the classics on library shelves. Because they were edited in this way, we, in our turn, are able to read them. These missives were also sermons, 'little sermons', in the words of one of the letter-writers, Adam, abbot of Perseigne. He was worried that, since he wrote in Latin, he might not be fully understood. 'I would have written to you in the language of the laity', he said to the countess of Chartres, 'had I not known that you were able to understand Latin.' There followed this advice: 'If there is anything here which is hard or difficult for you to understand, you have with you that good chaplain who will iron out the difficulties for you.' And in another letter, at the request of one of his correspondents, Adam copied out a sermon he had actually delivered before a 'community of nuns' for 'their edification'.

Large numbers of such letters survive, and we must be

selective. Most of them consist only of politics, institutions and squabbling. I will confine myself to those which are edifying, the letters of spiritual direction, and attempt to tease out of them how the priests of the twelfth century saw women, those sinners they felt it their duty to rescue from the clutches of evil. We must not forget that their deepest thoughts reach us in a distorted form. They are warped by the rules of literary expression, and by those of politeness, and by the anxiety not to offend but rather to flatter the recipient of the message, who was always a woman of high birth. Here, too, the historian has access only to the highest levels of the social and cultural hierarchy; the exhortations to do good all issued from very great men, bishops or abbots, and the women who listened to them were all or nearly all princesses, 'of a nobility of high blood', 'procreated according to the flesh by a royal blood and seed', the privileged 'parishioners' of the rulers of the Church.

The men who addressed them admitted that 'the female sex is not without understanding of profound things', that it was not made only of sensuality, and that 'keen intellectual liveliness as well as elegance and moral prowess' was sometimes to be found in it. This is what Hugh of Fleury said to Adela, countess of Blois, daughter of William the Conqueror, a very great lady of the Loire region, a focus of attention for all the fine minds of those parts at the beginning of the twelfth century. This concession made, half sincerely, these men all believed that women were their inferiors. In their eyes, the female nature was distinguished by two features, first *infirmitas*, weakness, and second, the burden of the carnal, which dragged them down. If they found strength in a woman, or one of the three other cardinal virtues, prudence, justice and temperance – which did sometimes happen – this exceptional advantage seemed to them to proceed from a blessing of providence, the indulgence of God who had placed in them a few grains of virility. When Bishop Ivo of Chartres wished to please Matilda, queen of England, he told her: 'God has introduced manly strength into your woman's breast.' St Bernard informed nuns that while it was admittedly rare to find *virtus*, force of character, in men, it was incomparably rarer in women, who were 'weak'; the younger they were, he added, the greater their weakness. Old age lessened their innate debility and also, happily, dimmed that suspect feminine attribute, beauty.

The priests inferred from this that women ought to remain constantly under masculine tutelage. It was not appropriate for them to exercise public power. If, by chance, because her husband was far away on a campaign, or had departed this world, a woman was obliged to take up the reins of power, she must overcome her nature, transform herself and, painfully, become a man. This was the case with Melisende, the widowed queen of Jerusalem, to whom St Bernard sent a letter of consolation in which he makes her say: 'I am a women, hence of weak body and unstable heart', the duties I have to perform 'exceed the powers of my understanding'. In such circumstances, what was needed was a conversion, a change of sex. Hence the prelates exhorted them: 'In the woman, you must reveal the man, and perform the task in a spirit of resolution and strength', two qualities that were, they believed, normally lacking in women.

The belief that it was necessary for women to suppress their femininity and make themselves masculine in order to withstand the attacks of the devil was expressed by Hildebert, bishop of Le Mans, in his letters to Adela of Blois. When he wrote the first, Adela's husband was alive but overseas, and for a long time, on crusade. The countess was steadfast. She managed the principality, not without difficulty, but competently. It was a miracle. So much merit in a woman 'came from grace, not from nature'. Without the special assistance of the Almighty, he told her, you could not have been 'the glory of your sex', and on two fronts, 'in that, though beautiful, you remain chaste . . . and in that, invested with comital power, you show clemency in its exercise'. This was a double victory over femininity, over that talent for seduction in women which led them into 'immodesty', and over that appetite for power which consumed them and which, as soon as they had occasion to command, made them 'cruel' (*crudelitas*: it was this same word that the priest, Lambert of Ardres, used to qualify the wickedness of Gertrude, the chatelaine he disliked). Adela had triumphed because the forces of evil that assailed her found in her a man. When she received a third letter from Hildebert, like all writings of this type intended to be widely read and discussed, and published for the instruction not only of this lady but of all women of her condition, Adela was a widow. She was leading a retired life in a convent. Hildebert celebrated the happiness she now enjoyed, since leaving the bed of a knight, a vassal and a subject, to receive the 'embraces' of the King. Once the wife of a man, she had become that of God. Let her not be afraid that she might be scorned or repudiated by this new husband because she was no longer a virgin or because, when she had been one, she had preferred a man to God, the knight to the Sovereign. For Christ was ready to join Himself to many women who had been given in marriage and consequently sullied. He took them all the same, and impregnated them in His turn; once past fifty, the partners of men brought no more children into the world, but those of Christ continued to give birth to those good works of which St Augustine had spoken. On this point, the bishop specified what made Eve and all women inferior: on the one hand, that lack which made the female sex more vulnerable, on the other, indulgence with regard to the flesh. 'The flesh plus the woman, a double infirmity,' said Hildebert of Lavardin, 'a conjunction which restrains them from renouncing pleasure' and diverts them from leading a good life, 'until age has put out that fire which proceeds from both the one and the other'; this widow, approaching the age when feminine charms inevitably faded, was told: 'If you feel the woman in you being rekindled and wishing to return to those follies', defend yourself; arm yourself with constancy. This masculine virtue grows stronger in women as they cease to be women. What the men of the Church demanded first and foremost from women was a victory over themselves.

The majority of the women to whom ecclesiastics wrote in the twelfth century were nuns. They were wives, too, but of Christ, and when the letter-writer was himself a monk, an abbot or the head of a monastic community, the letter was often a love letter; this love was *dilectio*, an impulse of the soul, absolutely pure, of course, a 'communion in charity'; it was a eulogy of *caritas*, that sweet and powerful bond which, according to divine intentions, ought to ensure the cohesion of the human race, bind it to the angelic cohorts and bring together in a perfect system all the elements of the cosmos. The man, then, in his letter, affected to bow before the woman, his 'lady', as he called her, which, in a sense, she was, since she was a nun, hence married to his Lord. And the posture adopted, the sentiments proclaimed and the words used differed little from those of the lover in the games of courtly love. The analogy is nowhere more surprising than in two letters written in about 1135 by St Bernard to Ermengarde, widow of the count of Brittany and now a nun; both are overflowing with emotion, exalting the union of hearts, celebrating this mutual and inexpressible love, which, said the abbot of Clairvaux, 'the spirit of God has implanted in the very depth of my being'. This was indeed love.

When, however, it was bishops addressing nuns, they were less lyrical and made sure that no one forgot that they dominated, paternally, admittedly, but firmly, the women they called not their ladies, but their sisters or, more often, their daughters. They were, in effect, in the position of a father who had undertaken to hand over one of his daughters in marriage once she was nubile. These women were entrusted to them, and they were 'promised'. Their husband awaited them on high, in the celestial city, where they would join him as soon as they were old enough. But this was not yet the case, so they must be treated like those young girls who, at this period, were engaged long before they were ready for marriage. The bishop took charge of them and guided them. The road was steep and difficult, but they must persevere, not lose courage, and above all neither stumble nor slip. They must remain forever on the alert, attentive to the most secret part of them. Do not forget, they were told by, for example, St Anselm, 'each of you has her angel, who sees every thought and every deed, who notes and reports everything to God. Let each of you, dear daughters, watch over the movements of her heart and of her body, as if her guardian angel saw her with corporeal eyes'; they were under a permanent inquisition, the gaze of another penetrating into the very depths of the person. The angel watched and spied without saying a word, but the bishops used words to warn, this being their job.

They warned against intractability, but above all against that warmth that invaded the body, that sprang from the flesh, from sex. Sex was these prelates' prime concern. How could one return to the Paradise from which our first parents had been expelled? By chastity, answered Ivo of Chartres, for whom the sin of Eve was clearly the sin of the flesh. For Hildebert of Le Mans, the primordial commandment was: 'Trample sex underfoot [first] and the vanities of the world, make the body a living host.' Daughters ought to offer their flesh as a sacrifice, and consume it. The injunction recurs with monotonous regularity. In the flock, the sheep are of two kinds. One group has known evil. These are the widows, now withdrawn into a convent, like Adela of Blois and Ermengarde. Some of them had been happy in the arms of a husband, remembered, and were unable to dispel the memory. This was where the danger lay, in 'listening to the sirens', in indulging in those surges, those recurring prickings of sensuality that tormented Héloïse, or in indecent dreams, consequently separating oneself from the celestial husband. He was indulgent and ready to accept them, too, as His partners, in spite of their lost virginity. But, like all earthly husbands, Christ obviously preferred them intact. Virginity brought honour on families and made fiancées valuable. This was why bishops preferred nuns to be virgins. They were especially concerned for them, fearful that they might lose their 'treasure'.

But many of them, the bishops were well aware and regretted, dreamed only of losing this treasure, and the sooner the better. For most of them were in the monastery as it were in transit, awaiting marriage; many of them had already been granted to the man who would come to take them once they had passed the age of twelve and were at last ready for sexual relations. Convents of women were there to protect child brides from accidentally being deflowered. One after the other, these girls left the cloister, set out joyfully, in procession, for the bedchamber of their husband. But those for whom their parents had been unable to find a husband remained behind, eating their hearts out. The prelates worried about them and tried to comfort them by the letters that were read out in their presence and circulated from abbey to abbey. To put new heart into them, Ivo of Chartres set out to persuade them that widows and wives were very much worse off than they were, since they wept at 'the irremediable corruption of their flesh, source of pain', whereas virgins, their bodies at peace, without fear, reposed in a serene bliss equal to that of the angels. With the angels of God, they were told by Hildebert, they sang 'the hymn of happiness that no one can express, except those who have never had bodily intercourse'.

The eulogy of virginity, constantly reiterated, was not enough, one suspects, to root out the seeds of sin from the hearts and bodies of those left behind, the sadness, the bitterness, the bouts of desire provoked by bad examples. Indeed, among the permanent virgins the bishop had consecrated, established for eternity in their *ordo*, at the highest level of the hierarchy of merits, there were some who, as soon as they could, rejected the veil and turned their back on the immortal husband to throw themselves, burning, into the arms of another, who was tangible and whose warmth they might savour in the short run. In one of the letters that I would describe as circular, written to prevent nuns from committing such an 'apostacy', St Anselm pretends to challenge one of these renegades, offering her what may seem to us strange advice. She had decided to become a wife, she had committed herself, she had already given herself. So what? Why not break this carnal and altogether worldly union. She could do it, there was still time. Let this young woman repent, let her trample underfoot her profane finery, and put on once again the dress of the fiancées of Christ. Christ was calling her. He would take her again, if not a virgin, at least chaste. She had fallen, obviously, but she might perhaps be able to establish herself higher than many virgins, 'if she renounced the world, if she scorned the man who had caused her to fall, who already scorned her, who, at any rate, would doubtless soon scorn and abandon her'.

It was better by far, however, not to take the risk, but to remain tranquilly in the fold, vigilant, subjecting oneself to a way of life liable gradually to destroy all bodily charms. There should be, above all, no baths, but an emaciated face, furrowed by tears, and a skin coarsened by a hair shirt. And the cloister was like a rampart against temptation: 'The walls of the monastery are built for this, so that those who love the world are not received into the entrenched camp of those who have fled it, so that you do not show yourself in public, exposing your body to infection. If you allow in the shameful reflection of what you have seen in the world, you will imperil your virginity.' Flee the conversation of men. Mistrust laymen, but mistrust the clergy, too. 'If capital punishment is the fate of the wife deemed to be an adulteress because she turned towards another man, what will be the punishment of she who, despising chaste marriage to the immortal husband, has carnally taken her love to another man?'

The bishops also went out on the attack and tried to put the nuns off marriage altogether. Married life was a terrible disappointment, said Hildebert of Lavardin in a letter to a recluse. That joining of bodies which the gallants claimed to be so sweet, 'that mêlée that takes place in the marriage bed provokes shame and disgust'. As for children, you are knee-deep in squalor and filth from the moment they are conceived; you risk your life bringing them into the world, after which it is all worry and drudgery. And as for the husband, were these young girls aware what female weakness might have to put up with from his caprice? If a wife was fertile, she lived a life of anxiety, if she was sterile, she died of grief. Constantly under suspicion as long as she was beautiful, as soon as she was not, the husband cleared off. To please this man and keep him, she had to resort to spells, those secret practices known to 'little old women'. 'I do not denigrate marriage', claimed the bishop of Le Mans, 'but I prefer repose to labour and liberty to servitude.' These were exactly the words chosen by Héloïse to extol ardent love, and the disinterested gift of oneself. But in Hildebert the intention is quite different. Liberty was virginity; by refusing marriage the woman remained mistress of her body, she was under no obligation to discharge her 'debt'. There was no stain, the flesh was silent, she was at peace, and soon there would be bliss, the true marriage, the only one that was perfect, the union with Jesus Christ. Before the virgins assembled under their rule, the bishops vied with each other to paint this mirage in the most glowing colours; happy the fiancées who proceeded, proud and wholly pure, towards the husband who, from heaven above, offered them His love (*amor* here, not *dilectio*). He awaited them in His 'royal bed', where He would take them in His arms.

In a collection of the letters of Arnulf, bishop of Lisieux, assembled between 1163 and 1181, there is one of consolation addressed to a young nun. It, too, speaks of a union, in this case earthly, between a man and a woman, but which the grace of God had just transferred from the bodily to the spiritual, transported to a Paradise rediscovered in innocence. At the age of seven, with the agreement of the two families, the little girl had been engaged to Arnulf's brother. As the time approached when the engaged couple would sleep together in the marriage bed, the boy died. He was lucky, said the bishop, since he had been first to enter the celestial couch. He was preparing a place there for his fiancée. 'Invited to the wedding of the Lamb, she would soon come to copulate there in His sight, and experience pleasure in joyful mood.' They make a surprising trio. The language is strong and the image it evokes is brutal, almost obscene. Arnulf continued: you, too, are lucky; you are intact and, as a result, the love which binds you is of an incomparably superior kind. There follows a meditation on love, a comparison of the two sorts of love, the one 'corruptible' and the other that is not. 'The love generated by the passions of the corrupt flesh is always liable to be corrupted. Irrepressible at the beginning, it is also quick to evaporate, and so completely that it is often transformed into hate, and its pleasures turn sour . . . there are many signs that it does not proceed from charity.' Whereas the other love grows stronger as it increases. 'In *caritas*, she who has become the wife of Christ does not commit adultery when she continues to cherish the fiancé whose carnal embraces she is spared. Continue to envelop him in a pure love, seek him, not by the eyes of the body but by those of the heart. God is not jealous of such a love'. This is the lesson that the bishop of Evreux believed it his duty to disseminate among amorous nuns under the pretext of helping an unhappy girl to choke back her grief, a widow yet still a virgin, her 'treasure' miraculously preserved by the favours of Heaven.

Until around 1180, bishops had generally written to the women enclosed in nunneries only to exhort them not to fret or to forbid and protect them from love. After, in contrast, it was love that was proposed to them, a love whose fires, when the loving fiancée appeared before the celestial lover, 'guileless and rubicund', would bring a warm glow to a cheek previously pallid from the languors of waiting. At the same time, Jesus was now presented to them as a real man, their companion for life. In childhood, their foster brother, He was from then on their leader. Let them follow Him, step by step, all the way to the Cross, to lose themselves in grief in contemplation of His wounds. Jesus is shown as above all the 'fountain of love', 'the sole consolation of women tormented by love', and the vocabulary and metaphors, many of them taken from the *Song of Songs*, evoke less the calm attachment of spouses than the passionate fervour of lovers. This is the case, for example, with those of Adam of Perseigne, whose letters are among the most vibrant.

Initially a priest, Adam may have served Marie of Champagne, daughter of Eleanor of Aquitaine, and thus known Chrétien de Troyes and Andrew, future chaplain of Philip Augustus. He became a monk at Marmoutier, then entered the more austere Cistercian order before finally, in 1188, becoming abbot of Perseigne, in the diocese of Le Mans. His great culture and the power of his language made him famous throughout high society. Richard Coeur de Lion chose him as his confessor. He was assigned by the pope to try to make peace between the kings of France and England. In 1195, he was in Rome, debating with Joachim of Fiore. He had close

links with the group of Parisian preachers inspired by Fulk
of Neuilly and Peter the Chanter, and in 1204 he took part
in the fourth crusade, leaving it with the more principled
participants, including Simon de Montfort, when the
expedition changed course. Until his death in 1221, he never
ceased to exert pressure through words. These words were
magnificent and widely heard, for his letters were copied
everywhere, read and reread in the monasteries and in the
courts. I will discuss one of them, written for the virgin
Agnes. It is in fact an edited version of a sermon that Adam
had delivered in a convent for women. We must imagine him
in the middle of a circle of virgins, sure of his ascendancy
over them, choosing his words and his images with the
deliberate intention of arousing their ardour, of making their
heads spin and of leading them, intoxicated, towards mystical effusions.

The sermon is constructed, as was customary, on two
verses from the Bible. One, taken from the Gospel of St
Matthew, reports the words of Peter to Jesus at the time of
the Transfiguration: 'Lord, it is good for us to be here.' Three
of the disciples are present, Peter, John and James. John
represents chastity, James humility and Peter, pre-eminent
since Jesus placed him above the others to lead them,
represents love. Adam calls him 'in love with love', and it is
he, 'friend of the promised man, guardian of the promised
woman', who must serve as the go-between, and seal the
couple's union. The other verse, 'My soul failed when [my
beloved] spake', comes from the *Song of Songs*, and this is
the real theme of the homily. Liquefaction and languor: love
penetrates the whole body like a fever, an inflammation of
which the seed is desire, the desire, clearly, for the other sex,
the desire for desire, cultivated for its own sake, born of
absence, and firing itself in expectation. It is an unquenchable
thirst, that torments the soul and makes it melt, not only the
soul but the mind, which itself melts 'of desire for pure love'.
After thirst, intoxication: 'The power of love either renders
you languid or intoxicates you', immerses you in perfect joy.
'Lord, it is good for us to be here.'

To attain to ecstasy, the loving woman – that is, all the

virgins who are there listening attentively, drinking in the
words of the director of conscience – is urged to follow the
same path as the heroines of the romances of the day. Here,
too, the fire is fanned by an exchange of glances, the sight of
the beauty of the other, then the exchange of words and
messages, the arms that hold and enclose, the lips that touch,
the coming together in a kiss. There follow, lastly, more
openly and, I would say, more shamelessly evoked than in
the poems of profane love, the pleasures enjoyed in bed. In
another letter, Adam had invited a nun 'not to be afraid of
sleeping with her husband, of tasting the joys of the marriage
bed'. Here, he goes further, and makes the listening women
penetrate the secrecy of the private chamber, guides them
towards the 'little flowered bed' all impregnated with the
odour of the loved one, and leaves them there to dream of
the 'mysteries of the marital bed', to inference, to that 'more'
that the troubadours modestly passed over, without dwelling
on it, in a single word. Whereas Adam harps on 'the tender
embraces, tighter and tighter, on the sweetness of the kisses',
on the movement of the bodies and, declining the verb
oblectare, on pleasure. This is the pleasure of sex, between
naked bodies. There follows this astonishing passage:
'Admitted to the interior, the fiancée comes close to the secret
of divine wisdom, she comes all the purer in that she is
naked, divested of earthly garments and bodily appearances,
to join herself in bed with uncorrupted truth.' Of course, the
heady 'copulation' referred to here is wholly spiritual. 'The
soul, in all joy, serves him she cherishes all the more closely
in that she does not hide her nudity from the nudity of his
innocence', and the *commixtio* that follows the exposition of
the revealed body is, of course, said to be 'without stain' and
'ineffable'. One wonders, all the same, how such words could
resonate in the minds and bodies of these women without
men. At this point, the heart 'fails' from the 'magnitude of
love', 'at the fire of holy love', and the 'tears of devotion' are
its visible manifestation.

   Here, around 1200, we see everything that from then on
and for centuries, in convent dormitories, in the cells of
recluses and in the houses of beguines, would characterize

the outpourings of 'holy women', predisposed by their female condition to mystical excesses. I note, however, one inflection, which seems to me highly significant. Pushing the metaphor further, Adam of Perseigne emphasizes his own relations with the young women he directs. When, instructed by his discourse, they reach the threshold of the nuptial chamber, he no longer presents himself as the *prelatus*, he who walks before and guides. His position is reversed, and he becomes the servant of the lady, like the courtly lover. He puts himself at the service of her who is at last to be joined to Christ. Entering the bedchamber for the wedding, now fully the wife of the Lord, of his lord, she now dominates Adam with all the power she has just acquired, to the extent that it is now he who appeals to Agnes. Defend the cause of the servant before the husband 'when you hold him in the most tender of embraces', that is, at night, in the most private part of the house, like the countess Emma of Guînes when, by her caresses, she won from her husband mercy for ill-used women. To speak in this way was to attribute to the prayer of nuns a value that Abelard, a few decades earlier, had been almost alone in doing. Women, devout women, were from now on deemed capable of helping men to pass 'from the antechamber to the bed of love', where they themselves were already installed. This is a sign, if ever there was one, of a promotion in the condition of women. I, and others, have sought for significant dates that would usefully punctuate the history of women. The end of the twelfth century is incontestably one such period.

The rulers of the Church also wrote copiously to princesses, but not, to begin with, primarily to give them advice or put them on their guard against their desires or to direct their consciences. The appeal to be moderate, and not to use their sexuality to excess, was never formally expressed. It remained implicit within a generalized, banal and mechanical admonition to despise the pleasures of the world, and moral exhortation was almost wholly confined to the proper performance of the duties of their estate. Great ladies were asked to make good use of the power they wielded, in particular over their husband. At the right moment, they should exploit their charms to soften the man whose head lay on their breast, to make him yielding, temper his brutality, lead him towards good, influence his soul, persuade him to love and fear God and turn his heart away from 'evil counsel', constantly returning to the task, choosing their moment, pressing their point. This was in itself to show confidence in femininity, and no longer to regard women as so wicked. It was to treat women as useful allies, whose virtues might help to correct the morals of men. In practice, these bishops and abbots, like the authors of romances and poets when they dedicated their works to princesses, counted above all on their correspondents to win for them the favour of their husband, so that he would do them justice or grant them some privilege or benefit. The majority of the letters addressed to the wives of powerful men were, in fact, petitions.

We should not, however, assume that the prelates were indifferent to these women's salvation. This was far from the case. From the beginning of the century, they had observed the disruption caused by the rapid progress of ecclesiastical reform and by the implementation of the rules of continence that were now imposed on all servants of God, and they had been faced with a social problem, that of the many mistresses of priests who had been thrown out on to the street and who were demanding help. At the same time, they were struggling to persuade the men and the women of the high nobility to accept a new morality of marriage. This led many if not all of them, such as Hildebert of Lavardin and, later, Stephen of Fougères, to ask what place God had meant to assign to women in the spiritual order. They set out to adapt their pastoral activities so that they would be effective in leading women along the right path. But reform was accompanied by a rapid expansion of female monasticism, and they saw their prime duty as lecturing the nuns, virgins or widows. When, like Bishop Ivo of Chartres, they took an interest in wives, it was primarily so as to prevail upon them to intervene to persuade their husband to respect the new rules they were in the process of laying down. A certain reticence prevented them from going further, in particular with regard to the sin that the fact of being a wife obliged a woman to commit every time the man to whom she belonged came to her in the bedchamber. In the ninth century, Archbishop Hincmar of Reims had believed that churchmen should not meddle in matters of this type. At a time when the framework of marriage was becoming more solid, it seemed natural to the bishops to leave to the husband, as long as he was on the spot and not separated by war or pilgrimage or death, responsibility for the salvation of his wife and for her actions. At the very end of the twelfth century, this reticence fell away. We see this in the correspondence of Adam of Perseigne, in three letters written for the benefit of three very great ladies, all of royal blood, the countesses of Perche, of Champagne and of Chartres.

Adam was their friend, in a friendship he called 'new'. By this we should understand not recent, but very different, in its vitality and frankness, from the conventional relationships hitherto formed between men of prayer and married women. The abbot exploited this bond of affection to extend his instruction beyond the cloisters into the courts. He went there himself, and he spoke there, for example at the 'colloquium' he arranged at the request of the countess of Chartres. This lasted for two days, and Adam was not alone with the lady but surrounded by all the female members of the household and by women from other households who had been invited to hear the good word. But he also directed consciences in writing, for example in the collection of little sermons he sent to Blanche of Champagne, and in the three letters he claimed to have written at her request: 'You asked me for them so as to encourage you to desire eternal things.' These missives, which were passed on by princesses to their friends and to the wives of men of less elevated status, were in effect responses to the spiritual expectations of women.

They were adapted, obviously, to the circumstances. These devout women were all rich. They lived in 'delights' while the poor suffered at their gate. They were legitimately rich, and necessarily so, so that they could live in a style worthy of their rank and exercise power 'as was required by their

high blood'. Adam's letters repeated, accordingly, the tra-
ditional themes: how to use this power piously and how to
please God in the midst of a sumptuous court, surrounded
by a throng of dependants and flatterers. So we find once
again the call for humility and for contempt for the pleasures
of the world. But the sermon has acquired a loftier tone.
Where these princesses were still in the power of a husband,
they were no longer required to put pressure on him, to
intercede with him in bed, whispering in his ear during loving
embraces. Adam asked nothing for himself or for his pro-
tégés. He spoke of the salvation of the soul to a person
responsible for herself, even in the most intimate acts. He
called on her to possess by possessing nothing. She should
not dispossess herself entirely, which would be improper, but
reject luxury and live frugally. For him, the symbol of the
superfluities that must be shunned was the gown with a
train. It made the women of the day 'effeminate', it turned
them into shameless little vixens, it accentuated what was
disturbing in the female body, image of that power of the
carnal that inclined them towards the dirty, image of vanity,
and image also of all the despoliation for which seigneurial
power was responsible. Such a profusion of useless fabric
ought to serve to cover the nakedness of the poor, not
carelessly, all dirtied, to sweep up the mire of public places.
In the midst of riches, she should meditate on social inequality. To revel in superfluity was in itself a grave sin. If they
gave nothing to charitable works, the rich were already
condemned, and the sin was worse if the riches were ill-
gotten, acquired through a misuse of power or, most of all,
of the capacity to levy taxes. Fiscality, a novelty of modern
times, was beginning to weigh heavily at this period. She
should care for the widow and the orphan, as kings ought,
not crush them with taxes; she should not seize the property
of the poor to pay entertainers, or to feed large numbers of
teams of horses, or load with finery 'that vase of excrements
that is the body'. A moralization of seigneurial exploitation
through the spirit of renunciation was the first theme. It
concerned visible attitudes; Adam went further.

To princesses who were widows, he prescribed a rule of

life close to monastic discipline. With the aid of a competent
domestic clerk, they were to read the sacred text and there
discover what they ought to do. Let them ponder how to set
about it. They should pray, seeking heavenly assistance.
Lastly, they were to strive to keep themselves as pure in the
world as in a convent. To achieve this, they needed a
steadfast faith. They should distrust false prophets, those
suspect preachers who suggested extravagant forms of
devotion. They needed 'innocence of morals', and to 'declare
war on evil desires', since it was in the body that sin was
found, in the flesh it was necessary to chastise. They needed
perseverance and, most of all, 'fear of God'. Everything
depended on this, since it led one to judge oneself, to punish
oneself now, rather than leave it to the Almighty to punish
in the hereafter. The fear of God led the spirit to disgorge in
confession all the evil on which it had fed. In fact, it was very
necessary to these sinners harried by temptations, much more
necessary than to the virgins protected by monastic walls,
that they should kneel frequently before a priest, examine
themselves, impose penance on themselves and beat themselves, since 'the pleasure of the lubricious body must be
mortified'. If these widows were able to turn their back on
the deceptive glitter of worldly luxury, conquer in themselves
that taste for sex bequeathed to them by Eve, choose
'mediocrity', and renounce in particular those jewels and
many-coloured gowns that were inappropriate to their situation, they would be rewarded. For them, the harvest would
be twice as abundant as for those women who were obliged
by the presence of a husband to have sex. They would receive
a third less than would be reaped by virgins, since they had
been deflowered and irredeemably sullied, unless, that is,
God took into account that they had been spoiled despite
themselves. Adam reassured Blanche of Champagne: 'Faithful in marriage' – he meant obedient, overcoming her repug-
nance, scrupulously discharging her debt – she was now
liberated. Once again, responding to the urgings of a husband
is seen, or at least presented, as servitude. Adam could go no
further. She might perhaps receive more. He hoped so, for he
was aware of 'the very fervent love she had for virginity

before the ties of marriage'. God judged intentions, not deeds. He would remember this initial purpose. She had not kept to it, admittedly, but this was because her parents had compelled her.

Adam spoke also to wives, women who had sacrificed their virginity, willingly or unwillingly, who were not yet fortunate enough to have been released from their husbands, were more involved in the frivolities of the world and so read the Bible less assiduously, and, however rigorous or generous their thoughts, were still stained by the simple fact of sharing the bed of a man and surrendering their body to his caresses. He did not ask them to restrict their expenditure or lighten the burden of taxes; this did not depend on them, they had no access to power. But he urged them to turn away from the things that were enjoyed in the courts. They should reject games of chance and even the 'subtlety' of the game of chess, much more so the excessive polish of courtly manners. They should hold themselves ready, and think constantly of death; its presence would restrain them from succumbing to the vanities. They lived, let them never forget, as in a dream, in the middle of a fog, which was denser the closer they were to the summit of power, and these 'fantasies' were 'almost always in the service of the voluptuous flesh'. It was important to dissipate these mists and see clearly, through faith, and through the hope and the charity that were stimulated by fear of God, but also through reason. Adam of Perseigne was a modernist. He knew the power of dialectic and used it to persuade, backed up by many arguments. He believed that women were susceptible to reason and capable of using it to defend their cause before God the Judge, with reference to right and to the law; he believed they were capable, by the 'tip of their intelligence pointing towards the light', of discovering truth. What they would then see was, first, the Virgin, she who, without being deflowered, had produced the flower whose perfume rendered the pleasures of the profane life insipid, even bitter. Contemplate her, take her in your arms, he told them. She who chooses Mary for her protector has nothing more to fear. But above all, if you resist guilty desires, you will become worthy of the 'most desirable sight of the loving Jesus'. 'If, for love of Him, you remove from the eyes of your heart the dust that offends them, you will see clearly what you ought most fervently to adore.' To these women, the least deserving of all since they were married, Jesus was suggested, as with the nuns, as the object of a passionate love. He is handsome, He is as good as He is handsome, as patient as He is wise, as humble as He is sublime – He is the perfect lover. Give yourself to Him, expel from your heart and mind what does not belong to Him. Your 'purified spirit will be led to celestial contemplation', even outside the cloister, even in the hurly-burly of the worldly life. Almost the only difference was that Adam did not summon the married women to mystical effusions, to melt. Only the virgins were promised marriage. Wives remained in sin and Jesus kept them at a distance. He showed them how to behave and, mercifully, He gave them hope, but He did not immediately welcome them into His bed.

The abbot of Perseigne had recently spoken in this way to the countess of Perche. He had started from the same basic precepts, exhorting her always to be humble of heart, 'restrained in appearance, sober at table, modest in expression, discreet in speech'. She should be open-handed and give generously what the poor lacked and, most important of all, remain chaste of body. She should seek above all to please the son of God 'who comforts you by the grace of the Holy Spirit'. You owe Him everything. To Him who has given Himself wholly to you, 'you owe all of yourself'. But how, he makes her ask, can I give myself wholly when I am not free, since, bound by the chains of marriage, I belong to another? The abbot replied with a series of logical deductions. He began by referring to the 'law of marriage' that God had promulgated in Paradise when he gave Eve to Adam as a helpmeet and partner. God did not oblige humans to have sex. He permitted them to do so, out of benevolence, bestowing it as a remedy. This was the function of marriage, to quench the fires of desire. And to be effective, this remedy must be based on what St Augustine had said were the three positive aspects of marriage. First, 'faith'. Let us be clear what this means; the spouses are at each other's service, in debt to each other; they do not have the right to refuse their body to their spouse, and they are bound to reserve it for them, after a contract very similar to that which binds the vassal and the lord; they are to give mutual assistance, even if it is very hard, and not to betray one another. Next came 'the hope of descendants', and the obligation to instruct in the mysteries of the faith and the knowledge of God what (*quod*) was produced by copulation. Last, the 'sign': forming a single flesh, the husband and his wife ought to signify the union between Christ and the Church, which is indissoluble. They are therefore forbidden to separate. That is the law. There is also the duty to 'deny the uses of the flesh' on feast days and at times of fast. These days are dedicated to abstinence in order that all the faults inevitably committed in bed would be washed clean by confession, prayer and alms-giving. During these short periods, the wife should live as widows should live.

That said, Adam sets out to show that a married woman could belong to God even as she discharged her debt in the arms of her husband. Christ appears here as that perfect man whose intoxicating splendour Adam had lauded to nuns in other letters, in order to arouse their desire and elevate them, by the ardour of their femininity, to ineffable joys. He tries to persuade his correspondent, and all the women before whom his letter would be read, that every wife was, in effect, shared, since she had two husbands, each of whom had rights over her. He starts off from the postulate that there existed a primordial distinction between the body and the soul, between the 'vanities', earthly dreams and fantasies, and the incontestable 'truth', which is in heaven. Throughout the demonstration, he sustains the opposition between *iste*, that is the carnal husband, and *ille*, the other, who is not called *maritus*, but *sponsus*. 'The carnal husband is the spouse of your flesh, God the spouse of your soul.' Of course, 'it is important to please the former', but do not forget, he said, that you belong to both. You owe a debt to each of them: '*Ille* claims His right in you.' It is a question of rights and of justice. 'God created the soul and the body which are both His by right. For the moment, He has granted the man the right over your body [that is to say, the usufruct, permission to use. The body of the wife was an object, a sort of fief, analogous to the property the lord granted to his vassal on certain conditions, or rather as a tenure, a piece of land to be ploughed and sown]. However, *ille* claimed the soul for Himself alone and would not allow it to pass under the control of another.' The obligations of the wife followed from this pact. She must be faithful and chaste towards both her husbands. Most of all, she must be modest. She owed the celestial husband the *pudicitia* of her soul, and the carnal husband her flesh, which ought also to be modest. She was obliged to submit this flesh to him, but she should surrender only it. Be careful, she is told: 'Do not refuse the heavenly *ille* His rights, on account of the earthly *iste*. When *iste* holds you tightly to him, enjoy yourself, take pleasure, but take pleasure in spirit, holding tight to the *ille celestis*.' If you succeed in this difficult feat, if you manage, in the transports of lovemaking, to dissociate yourself, and to divide yourself fairly, to give your body to one and your soul to the other at one and the same time, 'if you render to each his due, you will share in celestial justice. So, give your flesh, his right, to the man, but without depriving God of what is His. It would not be good for you to transfer this right to the use of another.'

The better of the two, obviously, is *ille*, the most noble. Generously, in taking her as His fiancée, He had presented His 'affianced' with a dowry which ennobled more than all earthly nobility, that is, the splendour of the angels, purity of soul and virginity of spirit. Considering the value of such a gift, you ought to reach out towards Him who gives it, contemplate Him, cherish Him and long for Him. While you are 'chained' to the man, 'obliged by necessity to obey and serve him, as long as he imposes nothing on you contrary to the law of marriage', it is He whom you should prefer. For it is with Him that the union endures. 'Marriage, which He instituted for the benefit of mortal flesh, is transitory. He gave himself as immortal husband to the immortal soul.' You should therefore first take care of that 'part of you by reason of which you are engaged to Christ'. In this, you are like the nuns, and, as firmly as they are, the wife is captive, bound by the strongest bond, that of marriage. Like them, she awaits the wedding, which will come. She should therefore adorn with her virtues the place of private intercourse, vigilantly preserve within herself a secret garden, a sort of cloister, a tabernacle, like a little wedding chamber, there to welcome the Spirit. It should be a 'consecrated' – the word is used – space in her heart, strictly forbidden, of course, to the man to whom she had been given by her parents, who had taken her, and who, at night, in bed, still called her to him and took her.

This is a remarkable text, for the rigour of its reasoning and the power of its language, but above all for what it reveals. There appears in the full light of day what churchmen believed about women's bodies and what they wanted women themselves to believe. The body was, they repeated a 'vase of excrements', at any rate the site of corrupting, restless sin, since our first parents, by the fault of Eve, were expelled from the earthly Paradise, through the uncontrollable impulses of the flesh. It followed that wives, those girls who had not preserved the integrity and the innocence of their body, should detach themselves from it and as far as possible forget it. They must surrender it, admittedly, to the man who solemnly received this perishable flesh, who took possession of it and who still burned to enjoy it. The union, the *commixtio* of the sexes, must take place. This was only right; it was the law of marriage and the duty of spouses. Ideally, this duty should be painful, and it was, physically, for many women of this period. In any case, the woman should do her utmost not to join in. She should remain as if of marble, tense, teeth clenched, and she should resist and refuse to let herself be overcome by pleasure.

Such injunctions singularly restricted the sphere of conjugal love, the love that, according to Jean Leclercq, was eulogized by twelfth-century monks. Admittedly, the words I have quoted were assembled in a Cistercian abbey, that is to say in one of the most austere sectors of the Church. But they were dispatched into the very heart of courtly amusements. How were they received? Many sources – the gossip reported by chroniclers, or the measures taken on behalf of wives who were too young, and were damaged on the night of their defloration by the overenthusiastic assaults of an equally inexpert boy, whose face they had never seen – suggest that many wives remained permanently closed and frigid. But what of the others? What did they think about that division between the celestial and the terrestrial that was presented to them as just and beneficial? God was not jealous, they were assured by the directors of conscience, but were husbands? What did they make of it? How did they tolerate the screen between them and their wife that the priests, by their admonitions, aimed to erect? Should we be surprised to see, at just this period, the threshold of the thirteenth century, so many signs of a marked dislike of confessors among the men of the nobility?

The letters of Adam of Perseigne were, as I have said, sermons, and widely heard, since echoes of the written word reverberated in all sorts of ways. The audience was, nevertheless, always confined within a closed and private space, the convent, the household or the noble residence. At the time that Adam was writing, however, preaching had become one of the main functions of the clergy, and the training of preachers the first function of the schools. From the Church, the urban church, the message was sent out and made public. The faithful who had assembled for a service, and especially the women, who were expected to repeat to the absentees what they remembered of the sermon, were strictly enjoined to listen carefully to the words issuing from the pulpit. To assist the men responsible for delivering these words, model sermons were composed and gathered together in collections. The oldest we are able to read are contemporary with Adam of Perseigne. They proliferated in the thirteenth century, and they survive in their thousands, an immense, confused and impenetrable mass, in manuscript. It is now some twenty years since scholars began to explore and produce convenient editions of these texts. They are, I repeat, models. The collections of sermons are practical manuals, what were then called 'arts', intended for professional preachers. That is why they spoke Latin, the common language of the clergy. The men who took their inspiration from these books transposed the contents into the dialect that their flock would be able to understand.

Like some of the letters of Adam of Perseigne, these sermons are constructed on the basis of one or two passages from Scripture. They offer a commentary, organized according to the method perfected a century earlier in the schools of Laon and Paris, comparable to that developed by the masters in their 'lessons', and to that of the exegetes who, reading the first pages of Genesis, had gradually refined the features of Eve, the sinner; starting with the words, they elucidated their significance and culminated in a concrete exhortation, how to behave in such and such a situation. The model sermon differs from the gloss only in that it is written for 'ordinary people', produced for simple folk, for laymen and laywomen. It was adapted to their way of thinking, and resorted to every device capable of holding their attention and of somehow arousing them from their torpor. It was therefore peppered with amusing little stories. This over-abundant literary production is remarkable for its mediocrity, first for its monotony: the experts who assembled these collections appropriated without scruple the words of their predecessors, content to alter the order here and there. It is monotonous and, above all, platitudinous: the stupidity of the 'examples', the brief anecdotes chosen by their betters to wake up the audience, is staggering. Though disappointing, these sermons nevertheless contain material that adds to the image of women contained in the letters of spiritual direction.

Like those collected by Stephen of Fougères in the *Book of Manners*, the sermons were intended, in the expression of the day, *ad status*, that is, for each of the different 'estates' of society. Some of them, consequently, are addressed to women. I will pass briefly over the model sermons for virgins and widows. They contain all the commonplaces of the epistolary literature. To virgins, they endlessly rehearsed the inestimable value of their virginity and the absolute necessity of expelling from their minds 'evil thoughts and morose delectation'. They must live shielded by the decent shame that would protect them from hearing or doing anything libidinous or dirty. They were also given practical advice, to work with their hands and to avoid laughter. They were to shun cosmetics, and those 'adulterous vermilions' with which prostitutes adorned themselves. And their bed should not be too soft. Widows were reminded that they must be on their guard against resurfacing memories, the emphasis yet again put firmly on sexual pleasure. What the preachers said to married women, however, merits more attention. At the beginning of the thirteenth century, they still avoided speaking to them directly. The sermon was addressed *ad conjugatos*, to married couples, that is to say, in the first place to the men who were responsible for guiding their wife. It showed them how to use her in a way that was decent, how to treat her in a manner that was pleasing to God and how to protect her from the sins that especially threatened her.

The *Ars predicandi*, or *Art of Preaching*, of Alan of Lille, who died in 1202, contains one of the oldest models, which is perhaps too scholarly to have been much used. It is, in effect, a little treatise on conjugal morality, based on the words of St Paul, 'to avoid fornication, let every man have his own wife . . . for it is better to marry than to burn', and it returns to the reflections of St Augustine in the *Contra manicheos*. They are briefly summarized. For marriage to be 'spiritual', that is to say, true, it was necessary for 'the flesh and the spirit to couple according to reason', and that 'the flesh, like the woman, should obey the spirit, that the spirit, like the man, should direct and rule the flesh as a wife should be directed and ruled'. Everything goes wrong when the flesh rebels, when reason is seduced, loses its head, and begins to fornicate with the flesh, when order breaks down within the man, and I say man, the male, because it seems clear that the *conjugati* at whom the exhortation was aimed were the husbands, and they alone, because only they were active. They alone were responsible for repudiation, for adultery and for that excess, as culpable as adultery, that sullied the sacrament when the husband was 'too ardent a lover of his wife'. Alan of Lille has nothing to say to her. She may be present, but whether she is listening or not hardly matters.

She is no more than an object, necessarily subject, as the flesh is to the spirit, as Eve is to Adam, and as the soft, the limp and the impure, in accord with God's plan, are subject to the rigid, the luminous and the strong.

The sermons of Jacques de Vitry were collected and completed in 1226. Jacques was a preacher himself, and a very successful one; it is possible that, to assist his colleagues, he recorded the very words he had uttered in public. However that may be, the treatment is much fuller. It has diversified, developing what was only sketched out in the sermons of Alan of Lille. It is at the very end of the collection, in accord with the hierarchies, that we find the sermons 'to the spouses', after those concerning the various categories of men. Manuscript 544 in the library at Cambrai contains three examples. Here, Jacques speaks directly to women. He imagines them before the preacher, gathered on the left-hand side of the nave, as numerous as, perhaps more numerous than, the men. He makes a pretence of hectoring and snubbing them: 'I see some of you groaning because I speak of the wickedness of women.' But it is still to the husbands that he directs his advice. They should apply themselves to 'governing' their wife better, and it is to help them to rule her with a firmer hand that the sermon alerts them to female failings. In the same way as Stephen of Fougères, Jacques de Vitry calls attention to evil in order to extirpate it, to purge the conjugal union of the seeds of infection that, once again, come principally from the wife.

Like Alan of Lille, he began by celebrating the 'dignity of marriage'. He started off from the Garden and the creation of Eve. Believing that carnal desire had tormented the man from the beginning, he thought he could argue that God had created a second sex in order to prevent Adam from falling into 'sodomitic lust or bestiality'. He gave him a wife, but only one, 'sufficient to assuage his sexual urge'. This was the task assigned to the woman. She, too, ought to be content with one partner, which was more difficult for her, because she was all ready and ardent, so demanding that men trembled and sometimes, inconveniently, went to pieces before her. Jacques now came to the rules of sexual good

conduct required of the couple. Because marriage was instituted to assuage the fires of sexual appetite, the woman
should never refuse herself. But nor should she 'feel she was
required to conceal her desire'. As for the man, 'he should
not behave violently towards her, regarding her as at all
times subject to his pleasure'. And 'if the wife can release
herself in some other way [from the excess of fever that
consumed her] without bringing scandal on her husband, she
should not tell him.' The priest, we observe, was pro-
fessionally well informed, perhaps because, after two centuries, the words of the *Medicus* regarding the remedies women
sometimes employed amongst themselves to bring themselves
relief had reached him. Was he indulgent, or disdainful? In
any case, he was discreet. 'There are many things,' he went
on, 'that husbands, who are too inclined to despise women,
ought not to know, and about which one should not talk
from the pulpit.' Ideally, an accord should be reached
between the spouses, each using their rights in moderation,
'in sanctity and in honour'. Be moderate, contain yourself as
far as possible, in the knowledge that marriage inescapably
contains an impurity, the pleasure one takes together, which
must be redeemed by alms-giving.

Since human beings are not as the beasts, since they are
constantly on heat, the 'honour' of marriage is threatened by
lust, in particular by adultery, 'which is the devil'. This was
far more serious when committed by the wife, because it was
then, in addition, a theft. Unlike men, women did not own
their bodies. If they were married, they were robbing their
husband when they gave themselves to another man, or even
when they simply light-heartedly scattered around the small
change of their charms, as women were too often inclined to
do. Jacques de Vitry had nothing, or almost nothing, positive
to say to these women.

He was anxious, certainly, to protect them, and urged
husbands 'not to revile or maltreat their wife, but to treat
her as a partner in bed [it comes first], at table, and with
regard to money, allowances and clothes'. They should not
beat her without good cause. All he felt it necessary to say to
wives was that they should look after their lord carefully,

keep house well, and bring up their daughters properly. For 'these days, you see many women who teach them love songs, who encourage them to run wild rather than to weep for their sins ... and when they see the little girl sitting between two boys, the hand of one down her bodice and that of the other up her skirt, they are delighted and say: "See how my daughter is sitting pretty, how the young men like her and find her beautiful", but soon her belly swells.' And lastly, there is the 'the primordial obligation, which is to obey her husband in everything'. They are equal, she and he, as to the flesh, but the husband is the master of the wife, vested with the power to 'govern her, correct her if she errs, constrain her if she is in danger of falling'. Such a dominion was very necessary, since evil came from her. 'Between God and Adam, in Paradise, there was only one woman. She did not rest until she had separated them.' Ever since, it is always wives who wreck the harmony between the couple. They are not only 'weak', 'lubricious', 'unstable' and difficult to keep a grip on, like pots without a handle, but unruly and quarrelsome. Beware of those who hit out, since this is the husband's job. For, by divine will, it is incumbent on the husband to rule, and first of all to control himself, not to become agitated like them. This is why Jacques de Vitry instructs the man, and the man alone. He feels concern only for him. Respectful of Mary of Oignies, the beguine, whose merit in his eyes was to have shrugged off her marital duties in order to give herself wholly to Jesus, he neglects the women who, for better or worse, accepted their status as wife. They had a husband at their side and it was up to him to train them and keep them in line. Let us see, next, whether we find a more generous attitude if we move a little further into the thirteenth century, and study the collections put together by Guibert of Tournai, who taught theology in Paris before and after his entry into the Franciscan order in 1235, and by Humbert of Romans, a Dominican, who died in 1277.

This time, we find sermons explicitly intended for women living in the world, and this is new. But in Humbert, it is almost all that is new. Like Stephen of Fougères and like

Jacques de Vitry, he accuses, rails against and violently denounces the failings of wives and their inclination to sin. He condemns them in order to arouse their shame and so facilitate the eradication of evil. His sermon 'to all women' begins, admittedly, with a eulogy of femininity, but in its sublimate forms, in its 'state of glory'. In Heaven, in Paradise rediscovered, the female nature comes into its own, he says, in the person of the Virgin. So women must prepare themselves, move closer to the celestial model by purifying themselves. And it is here that all the female faults are enumerated. First, there is their penchant for using spells. On top of this, they are without shame, talkative, idle and hard of heart. This very sombre preamble is followed by six models adapted to the different types of woman. Humbert hardly reproves noblewomen, as if blue blood was an adequate protection. Women of the bourgeoisie heard themselves reproached for their liking for money, which spoiled everything. When he came to the women of the household, the adolescent girls and the maidservants, he spoke to the mother of the family, urging her to exercise strict control over these potential sinners. She ought first to watch over the virgins, keeping them in a quasi-monastic state, apart from worldly things and, above all, well away from men, and she must introduce them to good books, those which told how to 'transfer all one's heart in the fervent love of Jesus Christ alone'. In sum, she was to make them into little beguines. She was to keep an even closer eye on the chambermaids, not so much because they ate too much in the evenings and got drunk, but because they incited boys to fornicate by the dirty things they said to them and by what they revealed of their bodies. How many young men of good birth, who did not dare go to a brothel, had lost their innocence in their arms? They were lost for ever, and it was the girls who were guilty for having offered them the apple. The last two sermons in the collection are directed at the lowest social levels. From the high ground of his respectability and his superiority of class, Humbert of Romans heaped every ignominy on this trash heap, the peasant women and girls. It was necessary to speak to them; Jesus spoke to the Samaritan woman. The 'poor

women of the village' had greatest need of Him, burdened as
they were with all the sins of the world, above all fornicators,
giving themselves to all and sundry, to the clergy, to their
parish priest, to passing monks. More dangerous still were
the prostitutes, but they, too, might be rescued from their
abjectness and saved. Had this not happened to Mary
Magdalen? She had been liberated from the seven demons
and redeemed by penitence, so completely that she holds
court in Heaven, most glorious of all women, except for the
Virgin Mary. A century and a half has passed and the tone is
unchanged. The men of the Church were afraid of women.
They were afraid above all of their sexuality. Humbert says
this explicitly in his homily to village women. Woman is Eve,
hence dangerous, not primarily because she is limited and
credulous, but because, like the companion of Adam, she
incites men to sex by offering them the forbidden fruit.

When Guibert of Tournai developed the theme in his turn,
he, too, denounced the perversity of women, their flirtatious-
ness, the excessive attention they paid to their hair and the
time they wasted in front of the mirror, trying to decide
whether to smile in a certain way, or half-close their eyes, or
which bit of their bosom to let be seen by choosing the most
flexible of fasteners. He still exhorted them to honour their
husband, that is to say, 'to do nothing contrary to what he
has laid down or said'. Nevertheless, this Franciscan is, to
my knowledge, the first preacher for whom the sexual act
does not seem to be viewed primarily as totally repugnant,
and who celebrated conjugal love before a female audience.
Of course, he prudently called on them to distinguish
between 'social' love (the basis of the 'partnership' and
'companionship' that developed within marriage) and
'carnal' love. For the purer love was, the more it was secure,
and the chaster it was, the more it was joyous. This type of
affection, therefore, should be encouraged. It could only
flourish in 'parity of intention', if the couple were equally
drawn to each other. So – and the homily is now addressed
to parents, those who arranged the marriage – one should
not, when forming a couple, bank primarily on physical
beauty (if one wished the couple to 'live together in honest

joys') or on wealth ('in fact, husbands ruled the household more strictly if they were not inhibited by the size of the dowry' brought by their wife). Marriages between equals were best. Then, the 'affection of love' helped them to go forward together towards better things, correcting each other. But, in any case, 'there are the appearances of love between those who indulge in vice [the vice is pleasure], and one may believe that in this friendship and love, even though stained by lust, there is a positive element'. This was a concession, though reluctant, but an opening at last, if timid, isolated and belated.

I have spoken frequently of the Church as if the ecclesiastical institution constituted a homogeneous body. I have said the Church did this or that, imposed its conception of marriage, and achieved, in this matter, its ends. To have written like this may have obscured the fact that the bishops, the abbots and the masters did not all share the same vision of the world, and in particular of sin. They had all heard the same lessons, they were all confronted with the same problems and all anxious to order social sexuality. However, the champions of virginity and those obsessed with the stain of sex coexisted with men who were less exalted, who believed that nature was not wholly bad and that it was sensible to allow a reasonable space to sex. Among the latter, there were many who mixed in the courtly world and who were anxious to develop a morality that would be appropriate to their family or their lay friends, and some of them forged the ideal tools to disseminate this morality widely. They preached in their own fashion, in the language of worldly gatherings, through romances, songs and the theatre. One of these men was the clerk who, in the second half of the twelfth century, I believe, and perhaps at the court of Henry Plantagenet, composed the *Jeu d'Adam*, a play performed at the beginning of Lent for the instruction of the faithful. There can be no doubt that the author was a man of the Church, like those who organized performances after him, since he reverted to Latin to indicate the stage directions in the margins of the spoken text. He had a good knowledge of the commentaries on the Scriptures, those of St Augustine in particular. Nevertheless, he portrays Eve in much less sombre colours. Admittedly, at the beginning of the drama, when he makes God speak, and shows Him explaining His conception of marriage to Adam, he states that the woman is subject to the man, under his 'commandment' and his 'discipline', and that Eve is the under vassal of the Almighty, since, subject, she must serve Adam, the immediate vassal. But he also makes God say that Eve is the 'peer' of her husband, the equal, and that she shares fully with him in the 'fief', the Garden of Eden, He had granted them. And above all, after the fault, when she succumbed, bewitched by Satan, too susceptible to the attractions of the fruit, to its beauty and the promise of its flavour, it is to the character of Eve that the author directs the sympathy of the audience. There is no allusion, first, to sexual sin. Then, before Adam, who heaps insults and reproaches on her, the woman appears by far the more dignified. God, she says, is her judge, not man. She submits herself to Him, bows down very low, and admits her guilt. She accuses herself, confesses, humiliates herself like a perfect penitent. She proclaims, finally, her hope: 'God will give me His grace.' She is sure of being saved, of already being saved, like Mary Magdalen, and by the power of love.

4

Love

It has been commonplace since Denis de Rougemont to locate in the twelfth century, and more specifically among the high nobility of France, what some have called the invention and others the discovery, or uncovering – *Entdeck-ung* is Peter Dinzelbacher's word – of love, or at least of the way of loving that distinguishes our culture from all the other cultures of the world. It is commonplace, but true: at this period, just when the structures of the institution of marriage, in the form desired by the Church and which would dominate for centuries, had been firmly established, there appear a number of reliable documents revealing the elements of a ritual that codified a new way of imagining, and perhaps also of living, affective and bodily relations between the sexes outside marriage. I say perhaps because all our information about these rites comes, in effect, from works of literature. These works were designed to please; they therefore transported the action away from the habitual, the everyday and the lived reality. How many true Lancelots and Gawains were there among the knights, or Guineveres among the ladies, or Fenices among the young girls, in real life? No one will ever be able to say. Only one thing is sure: songs celebrating the chosen lady and stories telling of the adventures of a lover and his mistress were composed during the twelfth century in the language of the courts, some were thought worthy of being put into writing, and many of these texts have survived. It is from this fact, and this fact alone, that the historian of medieval society can and must begin.

We may reasonably assume that the deeds and the sentiments ascribed to the heroes and heroines of this literature bore some relation to the behaviour of the men and women whom the poets were attempting to amuse. These songs and stories were enjoyed, otherwise their words would never have survived. Because they gave pleasure, we may be certain that they present a reflection of reality, and that the characters they portray did not seem so strange or fantastic that the knights and the ladies who avidly followed the progress of their love affairs could not recognize in them some of their own features or attitudes and, in their dreams, identify with them. To them, Lancelot and Guinevere seemed quite close. They were not inimitable and they were imitated; people played at imitating them. Like the lives of the saints, the literature of entertainment offered models. These examples were followed, more or less closely, and by means of this imitation, social reality moved closer to fiction.

It is also unarguable that the rules of the game of love were worked out at the courts of the greatest princes of feudal France. Did this happen earlier in the courts of southern France than in those that I have studied, a 'south' that was close, that began in Poitou, on the borders of Berry and the Bourbonnais? This is generally assumed, as it is suggested by the state of preservation of the texts. It is not, however, proved by it, any more than it is proved by the *razos* or the *vidas* of the troubadours, the explanatory notes that were fabricated 150 or 200 years later by the first editors, most of whom were Italian. Who will ever convincingly establish, for example, after the work of George Beech, that the 'count of Poitiers' to whom the oldest and the most beautiful songs of love are attributed was really William IX of Aquitaine, whom the monastic historians of his day accused of shameless and merry debauchery? Or that the famous countess of Die was really a woman? In northern France, the grip of the Church on high culture was much more exclusive, and for a long time this prevented people from transcribing onto parchment the words of the Romance dialects, so that they were simply memorized, but it seems to me unarguable that there, too, people sang of love at the beginning of the twelfth century. Abelard sang of his love for Héloïse, and he was a contemporary of William IX. And at the same time, other clerics, devotees of Ovid, were composing erotic poems in Latin, some of which have survived. No one, at any rate, disputes that, after 1160, writers perfected the model of the love that Gaston Paris aptly named courtly in proximity to Henry Plantagenet and to the counts of Champagne and of Flanders.

The development of the symbolism of love was rapid because the princes were competing with each other. Their glory and a large part of their power depended on the fame of their court. They were anxious to ensure that one could live agreeably there, and that body and soul were brilliantly adorned. With this in mind, they maintained the finest poets in their households. The princes also felt it their duty to educate the men and women who congregated around them. This was an old tradition; in the Carolingian period, the king's palace had been a school for good manners. The works composed by the writers whom the princes employed thus had a pedagogic function. They taught the customs that distinguished the well-brought-up man, the man of the court, the 'courtier', from the 'villein', the rustic or peasant. In particular, they taught the warriors how to behave properly towards the women they encountered in the princely entourages.

Lastly, the princes felt responsible for the maintenance of order. The Almighty had deigned to delegate to them His power and He expected them to keep the peace. One of their most intractable problems was restraining the turbulence of those warriors who, even if they were well on in years, were called 'young' because they were unmarried. They were numerous, since heads of families, anxious to avoid the fragmentation of their patrimony, saw to it that their younger sons did not produce a legitimate heir, obliging them to be celibate. These unmarried men, jealous of an elder brother, who, every night, rejoined his wife, were a source of discord in courtly society. They pestered the lord, demanding that he

give them a cousin or a niece or the young widow of a dead
vassal, for wife. The lord was unable to set them all up, and
most of them remained where they were, rootless, unstable,
on the lookout, ready to seize any prey. They did not,
admittedly, plan to take a woman by force, to abduct her as
one did in the ninth century. Rape had been succeeded by
seduction. The 'young men' set out to win the favours of
marriageable daughters, deceiving their families, or of wives,
deceiving their husbands. And wives, if we are to believe
Stephen of Fougères, were only too available, which was, in
Stephen's own words, the 'seed of war'.

For these knights, the great adventure, the heroic deed of
which they boasted as much and more than of carrying off
the prize at the end of a tournament, was not sexual prowess,
that fabulous talent for seduction exalted by some of the
songs of the count of Poitiers. It was to have enticed into
their arms a fairy, one of those strange and fleeting sylphs
whom the contemporaries of Burchard of Worms hoped to
meet one day at the edge of the wood, or, above all, to have
seized the woman who was most strictly forbidden of all; it
was to have braved the terrible punishments promised to the
adulterer and the felon and to have ravished the lady, the
wife of the lord. This was a double infamy, certainly, but a
dazzling demonstration of daring, the most coveted of claims
to fame. The fine writer who was assigned to compose
William the Marshal's eulogy reports that his hero's rivals
accused him of having seduced the wife of their common
lord, Henry the Young King. The author of the song seeks
neither to exculpate William nor to confirm the story. Was
the Marshal really the queen's lover? This perfect knight,
then a bachelor, was perhaps happy to allow doubts to
persist, proud that such a notable feat could be attributed to
him. But it was not without danger for the peace of the court
that seduction, crude or honeyed, was regarded among the
knights as a glamorous deed. It was a danger the princes
sought to avert. Without devaluing the exploits of warriors
eager to win the favours of women, they attempted to limit
the consequences by regulating them, by incorporating them
into the system of manners being constructed under their

control, and by giving them a strictly defined place within the culture of the court: *curialitas*; in the Romance language, *cortezia*, courtesy. They set out to contain the violence of sexual assaults within the framework of a ritual, that of a worldly recreation, the new love that was celebrated by the poets, a game.

It was a game, as we all know, in which there were three players: the lady, the husband and the lover. The lady was the main player. The authors of romances made her a queen. In fact, she was a wife, that of the lord of the court. As such, she exercised a threefold power over the knights. She was a teacher, since, as mistress of the house, she taught them how to behave properly there. She was a mediator, because she interceded on their behalf with the master of the house. And lastly, she was a seductress; her richly arrayed body was a focus for their desire. The lover, on the other hand, was unmarried and in search of adventure. All the young men recognized themselves in him. He incarnated their desires and their frustrations. He represented audacity and daring. His role was to capture the lady, overcome her defences and bend her to his will. Was the *senior*, the older man, the husband, consequently, mocked? By no means; it was he who controlled the game. He held all the threads in his hands and used them to confirm his authority over the 'young men'.

In fact, as Stephen of Fougères said, the lady was his honour. She was his glory, which is why he covered her with ornaments and displayed her. The lay of *Graelent* shows King Arthur, every year, on Whit Sunday, festival of spring-time and of chivalry, instructing his wife to climb on to the table at the end of the banquet and undress in front of the assembled barons; had they ever seen a more beautiful body? The significance of this symbolic undressing, according to Christiane Marchello-Nizia, is that 'the beauty of the queen and the appeal she could exercise over the vassals was simply one of the attributes of, and a way of exercising, royal power'. The wife was passive; it was not she who decided to strip. The man who held her in his power exhibited her, in the same way that, when he paraded his power, he had the pieces in his treasury displayed around him. He dipped into this collection of precious objects now and again for something he could give in order to make himself loved for his largess, and better served. The queen was the most brilliant and the most desirable of these objects. Solemnly, he revealed to the men who were his friends the secret charms of his wife. By making them this gift, he tightened his grip on them, since every gift demanded service. His wife, too, must be generous. It was her job to keep alive, by the meticulous distribution of favours, the hopes of the knights who surrounded her and dreamed of possessing her. In return, they served her like faithful vassals, and in this way they were tamed and gradually restrained themselves. The lady, in fact, was a lure in the hands of her husband, who allowed the game to proceed until it came up against the double prohibition of adultery and felony. It was he who was the chief beneficiary of this game. When the knight who served did his utmost to please his wife, was this not like a homage done to his own person? Was the knight not also, and perhaps primarily, seeking to please him and win his love? Was it not the case that the desire and the service of love rebounded from the person of the lady on to that of the lord? It is perhaps not going too far to see the strictly controlled amorous gestures performed between the wife of the lord and a knight of the court as in fact sustaining the love between these two men, a mutual love, the true and important love, on which was based, this time in real life, the vassalic order, that is to say, at this period, the state. This, it seems to me, is what emerges from this literature, the romances composed during the last third of the twelfth century, from which we historians derive everything we can know of courtly love at this period.

It may be argued that, in discussing courtly love, I am straying from my theme. This is very far from the case. I am seeking in this book to see more clearly how men of the Church regarded women. In the provinces in which I have carried out my research, the France of *langue d'oui*, the authors of chivalric literature were men of the Church. In the houses of princes, great and small, they served God, sang the offices in the chapel and heard confessions, and this was their prime function. But in addition, they introduced into profane customs the behaviour and the knowledge, the prejudices, the ways of thought and the image of Eve, an image of women, with which they had been imbued in the schools. They had all been there, and many left bearing a title, master, of which they were extremely proud. They were well educated, as is shown by the example of Lambert of Ardres, who served in a modest court. Skilled in discourse and debate, they read, wrote, knew the words through which to express the passions of the soul and translated from Latin passages of Holy Scripture, the periods of Cicero and the verses of Ovid with which their heads were filled. Thus they played alongside a duke of Normandy or a count of Guînes the role that the bishops of the tenth century had played alongside the Ottonian emperors. Stone by stone, they built *curialitas*, court culture, courtesy, by reusing the remains of the Christianized high culture of imperial Rome, of which the Church was the custodian. In the name of *honestas*, the virtue that made man worthy of esteem, they taught the knights, whenever they ceased for a moment to joust against each other, or chase through the forests in pursuit of game, refinement; they taught them to utter other words than oaths, rallying cries and the smutty jokes at which they guffawed among themselves, to behave better at table, and no longer to rush at women, but to try to please them. They passed on to them their own conception of love, one they had taken from their masters and their fellow students. They had not broken with the schools, and they knew how the word *amicitia* and the word *amor* were gradually acquiring new values, values of desire and of pleasure. They transposed these values into the poems through which the rites of courtly love are known to us. If, in the high society of northern France, during the course of the twelfth century, women were seen and approached differently, and if the ways of loving that the West 'invented' spread, it was to a very large extent, we too often forget, because it was through the intermediary of domestic clerks that what the theologians at Clairvaux, Chartres and Paris and in the monasteries, the communities of regular canons and the cathedral cloisters discovered in the domain of affectivity reached princely courts.

Twelfth-century Europe was experiencing a prodigious surge of growth. Everything was changing in the ways in which the use of words and phrases, and grammar and rhetoric were taught. Greater attention was being paid to the commentaries by the profane authors of the Latin world. What we call the twelfth-century renaissance, the growing veneration of ancient models, communicated, in addition to a host of images and formulas, a different conception of man and of his relations with nature and the supernatural. Everything was changing inside Christianity. The New Testament was being read more carefully and links with eastern Christianities were growing stronger. Journeys made through the countryside and towns of Palestine in which Christ and His disciples had lived made Jesus the man more present, and the theologians and moralists, meditating on the mystery of the Incarnation, and elaborating a doctrine of penitence, hence of responsibility, were tending to recognize that, in the human being, the flesh counted as much as the spirit. Everything was changing in the external world. A new fluidity was bringing traffic to the roads and encouraging the growth of all exchanges, and the spectacle of material progress was suggesting the notion that the march of time did not lead everything inexorably towards corruption, that man was capable of rising by degrees towards better things and that, in the course of his ascension, the fleshly part of him, too, might be magnified by joy. All these profound developments combined to disengage the individual ever more from the group, and to encourage people to regard the relationship of love as a free dialogue between two persons. Lastly, the finest scholars of the day, those in the vanguard, who led the flowering of thought, had not followed the same route as their predecessors, who had been placed when still very young in abbeys, citadels turned in on themselves, and knew nothing of the world. The new men had left the world only at the end of their adolescence in order to convert, change their existence, and enter a monastery like Bernard of

Clairvaux or put away their mistress like Hildebert of Lavardin. They knew what life was, and in particular what women were. All these changes and these experiences meant that, in three generations, the priests and the monks of the Ile-de-France, Picardy and the Loire Valley saw love quite differently from their elders.

They had seen it as a greed. If this desire was directed upwards, towards the spiritual and towards God, they called it *caritas*, if downwards, towards earthly things, they called it *cupiditas*. On this simple distinction was based the morality of good and evil and, in particular, the judgement passed on the way men behaved towards the other sex. Love was seen as an egotistical impulse, an appetite: it is for me, to satisfy my own lust, that I fling myself on such and such an object or such and such a person; like Eve when, hearing the serpent, she reached out her hand for the fruit. At the beginning of the twelfth century, a quite different attitude was beginning to appear in the Parisian schools. Love, good love, was no longer seen as a capture but as a gift. In the introduction to the *Theology*, Abelard defined it in this way: 'It is a goodwill towards the other, and for them, which makes us wish them to behave well, and this we desire for their sake rather than for our own.' The first reference is to Cicero, for whom friendship (*amicitia*, not *amor*) is a wish, that for the good of the friend, who is inspired by a similar wish. Commenting on Paul's Epistle to the Romans, Abelard went further: 'One cannot speak', he said, 'of love directed towards God if one loves Him for one's own sake, not for Him, and if we place in ourselves, not in Him, the purpose of our intention.'

St Bernard repeated and expanded this. Around 1126, his treatise *On the Love of God* describes the gradual sublimation of desire. In the beginning, man loved himself. The appetite necessarily took as its starting point the depths of the carnal. We are flesh. God made Himself flesh and redeemed it. It is the foundation on which all spirituality is erected. Then, climbing a degree, man begins to love God. At first, he does so egotistically, 'for himself', to appropriate Him. As he rises further, he begins to love God for God; this is the decisive stage since, as St John declared in his First Epistle, God is *caritas*, hence God, too, gives Himself. This leads into the final stage: man, as if consumed by the love of God, forgets himself totally, and merges into the object of his desire. He then accedes to the 'true' love that no longer has a cause and that, all lust abolished, expects no reward. His fruit is himself. 'I love because I love, I love in order to love.' This love is free and it is 'pure', 'all the more delightful and sweet in that what one may awaken to is wholly divine'. But how, despite the infinite distance that separates them, can the creature unite with his Creator, and in a love that is no longer accompanied by fear, a 'love ignorant of reverence'? It is possible because this love, like Ciceronian friendship, comes from a 'complicity of desires'; between friends, in parity, all hierarchy is abolished.

The demonstration has become much fuller less than a quarter of a century later, in the wake of sermons based on the *Song of Songs*, that celebration of ardent passion and all the marvels of physical love. This song was the subject of more commentaries in the twelfth century than ever before or since, testimony to the interest taken at that period, in the most advanced intellectual circles, in the relationship of love. St Bernard chose to base himself on the passionate words of the dialogue between the lover and the *sponsa*, the fiancée about to surrender her body to his caresses, the *amica*, the mistress, the girl with whom one took one's pleasure outside the ties of marriage. He did nothing to tone down the passion that shines through these words. Rather, his commentary further intensifies their erotic charge. For the aim of St Bernard was to excite desire to the point where it evaporated in the jubilation of the wedding. He traces, step by step, the progress of the amorous fervour: the looks exchanged, then the words that are 'confirmation of love', that avow and appeal. The appeal is to withdraw into a private place, to 'see if the vine flourish'. Do not be afraid, we will have plenty of time for 'that' (*id*) which we both desire, *pariter*, equally; there follows the kiss, then the embrace, and lastly the merging, the 'indissoluble fusion' from which 'joy spreads'. And the Shulamite, 'who is she? Us. Dare I say it, we are she'

– every human soul, seduced and wretchedly inferior to
'Him', that is to say, to God who holds out His arms. But
God also gives Himself. The union, therefore, is possible,
and the flow of joy mutually instilled. A fire rages: 'My
breasts burn with love'. *Adhaesio*, the coming together, is
here blast-off, an uncontrollable blaze, excitement and ferment, intoxication and vehemence. We recognize the words
used by Adam of Perseigne, a Cistercian monk, in his letters.
The disciples of St Bernard had, in effect, repeated them,
describing a fire spreading from the bottom up, and the
'attack' and the 'passion' of love as an access of folly.

St Bernard and his brothers were seeking a better understanding of what it was to love God. They themselves, and
other men of prayer, no longer as theologians but as moralists, were trying also to understand what was the right way
for a creature to love another creature, no longer to cherish
the unknowable but to cherish each other, in an orderly
manner, in universal harmony. They used the same terms,
amor, *amicitia*, terms whose meaning was immeasurably
exalted by all these meditations and arguments and the
passionate striving towards the divine. They used them
without hesitation to construct a model of affective relations
between two men. In his *History of the Lords of Amboise*, in
order to demonstrate the exemplary nature of the relations
that, from generation to generation, the heroes of his story
had maintained with their lords, the counts of Anjou, the
author spoke naturally of *amicitia*, and to demonstrate how
close and fruitful this attachment had been, he drew, with
the aid of many quotations, on what had been said on the
subject by the Latin authors, in particular Cicero. Nevertheless, it is the word 'love' that constantly recurs when they
wish to demonstrate the warmth of heart that united companions in battle, and that ought to bind vassals to the man
before whom they had knelt, and who had taken their hands
in his own. This is the case in the song of William the
Marshal, from which women are almost entirely absent. And
when, in one of the stories that has Tristan as hero, the
barons of England press King Mark to marry in order to
produce a legitimate heir, he replies that he already has one,

his nephew, his sister's son, whom he loves more than a son. And to define the tie that binds him to this boy, he speaks of love; he had loved Tristan from the moment he had seen him; a single glance had lit the flame in his heart. Addressing Tristan, he says: 'for love of you, I wish to remain throughout my life without a wife. If you are faithful to me as I will be faithful to you, if you love me as I love you, we will live our lives together happily.' We see here forcibly expressed the dream of a military society which would remain entirely masculine, and which would have no more need of women. Among the knights of the twelfth century – as within the Church – normal love, the love that caused one to forget oneself, to surpass oneself in mighty deeds for the glory of a friend, was homosexual. I do not mean that it necessarily led to physical complicity, but it was very obviously the love between men, strengthened by the values of loyalty and service drawn from vassalic morality, that was seen as the basis of order and peace, and it was to this that the moralists naturally transferred the new fervour with which the speculation of theologians had impregnated the word *amor*.

When, on the other hand, men of the Church were concerned with the relations between men and women – and this was one of their chief preoccupations, since they were trying, at this period, to construct an ethic of marriage and strengthen the framework of the conjugal union, the only place, according to them, where licit heterosexual relations might take place – they were extremely cagey. This was because, in this case, sex necessarily intervened, and because sex was sin, the stumbling-block. They were impeded by images – that of an excessively sensual Eve, and that of the chimera, the bugbear conjured up by Bishop Marbode of Rennes – and by that widespread obsession that made St Bernard, so susceptible to the charms of the Shulamite, unable to conceive that, in the sects in which men and women came together to pray, they were capable of spending the night in each other's company without falling on each other in disorderly, blind and bestial copulation. For the priests who were struggling to reform morals, marriage was above all a mastery of the bodily impulses, a bringing to order. Married people constituted one of those 'orders' whose harmonious assembly supported the equilibrium of society as it had been established by God. The 'order of spouses', like that of widows, and like that of the servants of God, ought to be structured by a morality made up of obligations and constraints. This morality had to be particularly strict because marriage had the function of procreation, because this was the consequence of a sexual conjunction, and because such an act could not be without stain. This was also being proclaimed at the end of the twelfth century, and very vehemently, by the Cathars, the most dangerous of the heretics. They, consequently, condemned marriage, whereas the rulers of the Church aimed to make it the basis of lay society. They set out, therefore, to find a way of reconciling purity and the sexual act. Alan of Lille had a shot. 'We have to accept', he said, 'that marriage cannot be consummated without coitus. Coitus, however, is not always sinful, since the sacrament means that bodily commerce is not a grave sin, and even that it is not a sin at all.' On condition that, in this commerce, neither of the two partners loses their head and lets themself be overcome by pleasure, on condition that both of them hold back. Continence was the answer. All the emotive words used by St Bernard to describe the exaltation that followed from the union of the soul with God, words like 'intoxication' and 'vehemence', no longer found favour. The moralists could not speak of abandon or effusion, they spoke instead of reserve, and of duty, not of gratification. Alan of Lille repeated the words of St Jerome: he 'who loves his wife with too much passion is an adulterer'. The spouses were expected to discharge their 'debt', but they should as far as possible do so without enjoying it; the sin lay in sexual pleasure. It was a sin, said Peter Lombard, to expect from one's wife the pleasure that one found in the arms of whores; moderation, the effort of temperance, obliterated the greater part of the evil, and what remained could be redeemed by long penances. The prohibitions, we should note, were invariably addressed only to the husband. It was his responsibility to hold back and, above all, it was up to him to repress the excessive passions of his wife. For, as everyone knew, the female nature was 'inflamed by the furious torches of the libido'. As, according to Orderic Vitalis, were those Norman wives whose husbands lingered in England, who tired of pining and threatened to go elsewhere to calm their excitement. And Jacques de Vitry and many others heaped praise on the prowess of those husbands who were so well able to restrain their lust that they never touched their wives, like the husband of Mary of Oignies and like Joseph, husband of the Virgin Mary.

Around 1140, Hugh of Saint-Victor meditated on the virginity of the Mother of God, and this led him to spell out the form that married love should take. Mary and Joseph were bound by a pact, whose clauses they must respect. This pact constrained them not to refuse each other. Could Mary remain intact while performing her duties as wife? Yes, replied Hugh, because the 'office', the prolific function of marriage, which required the union of bodies, is secondary, subordinate with regard to what is essential, that is the 'association', that *adhaesium* of which Adam became aware when, emerging from his torpor, he discovered the woman by his side. Such an attachment, analogous to that which bound the son to his parents, and which was loosened when he took a wife, could not be carnal; it was of the order of sentiment, it was born of a 'disposition of the heart', and it was strengthened by *dilectio*. This was the term used by St Paul in the New Testament to characterize the union of Christ with His Church. Of such a union, which was spiritual, marriage was the 'sacrament', the sign. It reproduced it. In one of his *Sentences*, Hugh admits that because marriage is a sacrament, the fault of the married couple was slightly reduced 'when they burned with love'. But this is in order to warn his readers to beware of a reprehensible excitation. There is nothing in common, in fact, between *dilectio* and *amor*, which is eaten up with lust. Nor is *dilectio* the same as *amicitia*, because, although there is a gift of oneself, there is a lack of parity. The husband holds the place of Christ, and Christ is incontestably the master. Hugh emphasizes inequality in the conclusion to his treatise. By the 'disposition of the heart', the husband ought to adopt with regard to his wife an attitude which strongly resembled compassion, if not condescension. Over this weak being who is entrusted to him, he leans, and he envelops her in his chaste tenderness. Whereas she, by the 'necessities of her condition', that is by the debility of her nature, can only let herself be loved by her lord, passively, in the perfect modesty of a 'loving partnership'.

The monks who offered the clergy the fruits of the reflections they had pursued in the silence of Cistercian cloisters, the masters who interpreted the sacred text before future bishops, all the men who, in the twelfth century, were seeking to reform the conduct of the laity and who, for the most part thought only of laymen, thus suggested that four radically different categories should be distinguished in what we call love. They put aside one of them, which they called 'fornication', a simple physical relief, the emission of semen. They regarded it as no more serious than a wet dream if the partner was neither a nun nor a married woman, or if the services of a professional, a prostitute, had been called on. Passing quickly over this contemptible act, they called for three degrees to be recognized in the sentiment of love. At the highest level was the love that was 'pure', as St Bernard said, a devastating fire, a concoction, a transmutation, liberating the quintessence from carnal desire in order to offer it to God. Next, less violent though still very warm and not devoid of tenderness, was love-friendship, or rather loving friendship, that which gave masculine society its cohesion. Lastly, there was the reasonable, measured, barely lukewarm affection that should exist between spouses, an 'honest and sweet feeling', capable, as the marquise de Merteuil would later write to Mme de Volanges, 'of rendering the conjugal tie more attractive and of, in a way, sweetening the duties it imposes'. For, in the matrimonial bed, and this time it is Montaigne who would repeat it, pleasure should remain 'reserved, serious and mingled with some severity'. Is it not the case that, in all the cultures of the world, marriage, basis of the social order, is too serious a matter not to be protected against the squalls of love?

This, then, is what had been said to the chaplains and the clerks who, in princely households, helped to keep the knights peaceable and who, to this end, from the middle of the century, adapting the stories they had read in the Latin authors and what had reached them of Breton and eastern legends, related the adventures of Tristan, Yvain and Cligès. Their employers demanded that they create a space between fornication and marriage for the playing of that complex game that they hoped would accustom the knights to restrain a little their virulent desire to ravish, the women to allow themselves to be courted without falling and the husbands not to behave too jealously. These poets borrowed from pure love, the love of God, its vehemence and its gratuitousness. The love between warriors and the duties of loyalty and service it implied showed them how, inverting the natural hierarchies, to place the lover, briefly, in a posture of humility before his chosen lady. But they also made a space for pleasure, the carnal pleasure the moralists aimed to eliminate from marriage. Drawing on the old habits of concubinage inherited from barbarous times, and that their travels in the Holy Land and Spain had revived among the itinerant knights, they gave their female characters some of the features of the 'mistress', the pretty girl who was ready to join in joyous libertinage. They listened, lastly, to the troubadours and, at the heart of the pedagogic discourse that was expected of authors of romances, there was an appeal to control desire and to stimulate it to its climax, a desire focused on a specific object, the body of the lady, the 'white, plump and smooth' body extolled by Bernard of Ventadour.

The rituals of courtesy allowed the young cousins and young friends of the master of the house to take this body, imagined under its garments, in their arms when the lady received them and when they took their leave, but they longed not only to touch it beneath the mantle and see it naked, but to enjoy it. Was this a totally unrealistic dream? What we can glimpse of courtly society suggests not. The lays of Marie de France imply that the ladies of this period did not always remain obdurately hardhearted. Among the songs in the *langue d'oc*, it is, significantly, those attributed

to married women that show the ardour of lovers easily
satisfied. And when Stephen of Fougères, expressing the fears
of husbands, reproached wives not only for letting themselves
be vanquished, but for meeting their victors halfway, these
fears were surely not without foundation. Nevertheless,
wives, whether they liked it or not, were strongly defended,
surrounded by stout ramparts. First, the material defences:
where could one find, inside the house or out in the garden,
a suitable place, where one could feel 'at ease' and avoid
being seen? The love literature is never so close to the lived
reality as when it describes youthful lust constantly thwarted
by peeping Toms, intruders, the jealous or *losengiers*, false
friends. We see the heroes of romances obliged to crouch
down, press themselves into corners and lurk in the shadows
for embraces that were always fleeting and threatened. Much
more to be feared was the irredeemable moral condemnation
of adultery, the gravest of female faults, on the part of both
warriors and priests, and the generally accepted right of
husbands to kill, even burn, their wife on the slightest
suspicion. In fact, the songs and the romances, a literature
designed for men, whose heroes are all men, and whose
female characters have never more than minor parts, foils for
masculine excellence, were constructed on a contradiction,
the conflict between law and desire. The poets of the *langue
d'oui* struggled to resolve this contradiction. They were men
of the Church and, in the words of Michel Zink, 'they
accepted less easily and less innocently than the troubadours
the incompatibility between courtly love and Christian
morality'.

They attempted to reconcile the two by shifting the gratification of desire into the unreality of the liturgies and
sacrality. Chrétien de Troyes does this in *Le Chevalier de la
charrette*. The room in which Lancelot at last joins the queen
takes on the air of a sanctuary, the bed of an altar, and the
lover bows before the desired body as before the relics of a
saint; he 'adores' it, as for so long, before receiving his
reward, he had adored the lock of Guinevere's golden hair
that he kept next to his heart, 'between his shirt and his
flesh'. The authors of romances wanted to justify sexual

desire by exalting *amor purus*, the 'fine' love of St Bernard,
disembodied or, more accurately, restricted to that very
private and ardent part of the person, the heart, crucible of
all energy, a sort of still where desire was clarified of all
carnal dross. In the recastings of *Girart de Roussillon*, a
bond of this sort unites Girart to Elissen, the woman who
was promised to him, but who, when the engagement was
broken, became the wife of another, an adulterous bond,
admittedly, but resolutely chaste. The game of love might
safely be played if one separated the heart of the lady from
her body, the body that she was not free to withdraw from
the seisin of her husband, and which it was a felony to take.

Such a division did not make for an easy life. This was one
of the lessons of the *Tristan* of Thomas. Adulterous love was
not happy. The love of the heart and the love of the body
could only come together in order and tranquillity within
marriage. In the last decades of the twelfth century, the
Church had succeeded in imposing its conception of marriage, the expansion of the monetary economy was making
the heads of noble households less reluctant to give a wife to
several of their sons, and the turbulence surrounding the
'young men' was gradually, as a result, diminishing; it was
therefore quite natural that the Romance literature, that
mirror held up before court society so that it would discover
not its real features, but the image of what it ought to strive
to be, would put free love into the context of marriage. It
was a prelude to the wedding. In *Cligès*, the anti-Tristan of
Chrétien de Troyes, it is the queen herself who gives this
advice to the young Alexander and the young Soredamors:
'It seems clear to me from your face that of two hearts you
have made but one . . . do not be foolish in your love. Join
yourselves together honourably in marriage. In this way, it
seems to me, your love will endure.' Love, pure love, was a
preliminary that prepared the bodies, and in particular it
prepared the body of the future wife to offer itself and to
become as 'delectable' an object as that of the mistress. In
this young literature, the heroine takes on a different persona.
She becomes the promised virgin, the new wife whose
husband expected her to shudder in his arms despite the

exhortations of the strictest directors of conscience. Both of them were happy. Chrétien de Troyes offers an exemplary image of such happiness, in that of Erec and Enide:

> Together they lie in bed,
> each embraces and kisses the other,
> and there is nothing that gives them so much pleasure.

But Chrétien was not deaf to what was being taught by the masters in the cloisters of Saint-Victor and of Notre-Dame, in Paris. He was well aware that, in marriage, love ought not to gorge itself, that the husband ought to be moderate. At one point, Erec forgot this. Too 'vehemently a lover' of his wife, he lost his way, he became deranged, he was no longer a man. Exhausting himself in an excess of voluptuous pleasure, he ceased to be 'the master of his wife'. It needed a series of ordeals, shared by Enide, to make him come to himself and revert to his masculine role and to the type of love which was proper between spouses. When the couple found each other again and 'swiftly they rode off through the night/the bright moon lighting their way', they embraced once more, and hugged and kissed, but this time under the control of that 'affection of the heart' celebrated by Hugh of Saint-Victor. Once the gulf separating married love from fine love had thus been filled in, courtly society joined whole-heartedly in the game. This may have been in part a consequence of a promotion of women. But it was above all a result of all those changes that were modifying men's behaviour, their interests and their desires; men were yet again the only ones to matter.

Towards the end of the twelfth century, perhaps in 1186, a remarkable book was completed in Paris, a treatise *De amore* (*Of Love*), or *De honeste amandi* (*How to Love Honourably*). Its author, Andrew, was a man of the Church. It seems that he had begun his career at the court of Champagne, close to the countess Marie, that daughter of Eleanor of Aquitaine to whom poets dedicated their works in order to please her husband, the powerful Henry the Liberal; she is supposed to have provided Chrétien de Troyes, in 1174, with the theme of his romance *Le Chevalier de la charrette*. However, when Andrew completed his treatise, he was, he says, 'chaplain of the royal court'; he had switched to the service of the king at the period when his uncles of Champagne, in order to keep him more firmly under their control, were placing close to him men on whom they could rely. Alfred Kernein has established that the Chaplain served in the chancellery. His treatise appears in the inventory of the oldest administrative registers preserved in the tower of the Louvre, and that it should have found a place in this treasury of books is clear evidence of the attention it attracted. It is dedicated to Walter, son of Walter the Chamberlain, the custodian of these manuscripts, perhaps because it was not possible to dedicate it directly to the king. Philip Augustus was not old in 1186, but, married and soon to be a father, nor was he, in the precise sense of the term, 'young'. Whereas Walter, like Lancelot, and like Tristan when he met Iseult, was a young man. Wounded by the darts of love, a love shown from the outset as a brutal aggressor, he had just become a 'knight' of love. 'A new recruit', not yet knowing how 'to manage the reins of his horse', he had asked the master for instruction. Andrew composed for him an 'art', a collection of practical formulas from which the apprentice would learn his trade. But the *De amore* is much more than this. It is a part of a general education. Its author places love among the disciplines required by a good manly training. Just as the knight strengthens his body, keeps it supple and tests his courage in the violence of the hunt and the tournament, and just as he improves his linguistic skills in debate and discussion, and furnishes his mind by listening to someone reading aloud, so, by engaging in love, he learns to master the tumult of his desires.

Andrew the Chaplain gives many definitions of love. It is, he says at the beginning of the work, 'a natural [that is, subject to the laws of nature] passion [an emotion, an agitation of the being] that results from the sight of the other sex [Andrew does not discuss the love-friendship that developed between warriors; further on, he declares: "Love can exist only between persons of different sex", because "it is ashamed to accept what nature forbids"] and from an obsessive meditation on this beauty [a visual sensation is the source of a turbulence that invades the mind, which can no longer detach itself from the material and corporeal object whose attractions it has discovered].' These features, the violence of the *impetus*, the shock, and of the fervour to which it gives rise, and that nothing can suppress, and avidity, lust and a fierce desire to enjoy a very obviously sexual prey, are emphasized in a second definition: 'Love is the frantic desire to enjoy passionate embraces.' The individual is here presented as captured, driven mad by the appetite to conquer, which Andrew the Chaplain further emphasises, basing himself on etymology: 'This word *amor*', he explains, referring to Isidore of Seville, 'derives from the verb *hamare* which means to catch or to be caught.' Or to be hooked; the vocabulary is that of fishing: *hamus* is the *hameçon*, the hook. Man is hooked by love, he is caught, or he catches it like an illness. It is passion, an end to restraint, a madness; it is a torrent, a terrible power. Is love therefore an evil? Not at all; it is the source of every good. The loving impulse is natural; it should not be eradicated at all costs, wiped out, as the rigid moralists wanted. When controlled and mastered, its power leads to self-fulfilment. Like the paladins of the romances during their initiatory wanderings, the young man who becomes a knight of love faces a series of ordeals. If he surmounts them, he emerges strengthened from the adventure. For, like friendship, love encourages generosity and largess and, like marriage, it is a cure for lustful, delirious greed; it focuses the desire to capture on to a single object, on to one woman alone ('he who is aglow with the light of love can scarcely contemplate the embraces of another woman, however beautiful'), and lastly, love inspires one to surpass oneself in order to earn the favours of the loved one, the woman who judges, certifies prowess and distributes the rewards. Love is king and Andrew shows it crowned with gold. 'From it derive, everyone knows, all the good and the courtesy in this world.'

These two words, *in mundo*, are crucial. Andrew the

Chaplain employed them to define the sphere within which he had chosen to confine his thesis, that of 'worldly' things. The lessons he dispensed concerned only one of the two domains that are separated, in the whole of creation, by the fundamental division between the sacred and the profane, the flesh and the spirit, *cupiditas* and *caritas*, Heaven and Earth, the world and whatever cuts itself off from and despises it, between the area ruled by divine law and that other area whose government God had abandoned to the laws of men and nature. Worldly love, the love of men and women, was a source of good because it was a 'natural passion'. Like Bernard Sylvester, Andrew was one of those scholars who were fascinated by all the progress that, before their eyes, was transforming the 'world'. He regarded nature as good and saw in it the zealous and fruitful assistant to divine will. He could thus assert that a man gradually became valiant when he submitted to the demands of the practices of love.

He took pains carefully to circumscribe the sphere of these practices, too. It was first a question of timing: one did not make love at any age. It was a mistake to begin too early; though boys were declared to be nubile at the age of fourteen, they should be patient and wait four more years before launching into amorous adventures. Nor should one go on for too long. A time came when, all benefit gained from the ordeals, it was wise to retire and to renounce love. The treatise contains three books. The first explains what love is and how to acquire it, the second, how to live it, and the third teaches how to be free of it. This section argues the opposite of the preceding books, and some believe it to be phoney. The evidence suggests, however, that it is nothing of the sort. First, it appears in Ovid's *Art of Love*, which is its model; then, the rules of dialectic, faithfully observed throughout, require that the two sides to a question be compared: after the good side, the bad, after *pro*, the exaltation of the amorous quest, *contra*, its depreciation; above all, in this educative manual, the route leads ever upwards. By degrees, the pupil is led towards better things, from the base and the carnal towards the spiritual. Like the first exercises in riding for the horseman, and like those in grammar for the man of letters, the game of love was only a stage in the journey that led towards masculine perfection, an indispensable stage, but only temporary. He who believes he is now well versed in this game, and in the type of manoeuvres it requires, he who holds with a firm hand the reins of his mount and makes it pirouette at his pleasure, is required by a concern for himself to go further, as far as that platform from which, from the height of the second stage of life, the vanities of the world can be seen.

It is also a question of space, social space: love is not practised 'honourably' on all terrains. Some, both men and women, are excluded from the game by their condition. This is the case, first, with those who are subject to divine law. Andrew does not even mention the most obvious of these, the monks, for they have already joined the angels. But he discusses nuns and clerics, because they are vulnerable. Love, profane love, is sufficiently fiery to break down barriers and spill over into the field of the sacred. So Andrew warns those he is educating to be careful of nuns; do not touch them; never remain alone with them. 'If one of them finds the circumstances propitious for wanton games, she will have no hesitation in doing your will, in abandoning herself to burning caresses.' The clergy are less quick to get carried away; they are men and they master their passions better. For this reason, the Chaplain calls them 'most noble', endowed with that eminent dignity conferred by sexual purity. Let them not forget it and let them take care not to slip up. 'Nevertheless, as there is no one who lives his life without committing the sin of the flesh', and as the clergy are 'more exposed to temptation than other men because they enjoy uninterrupted leisure and eat well', if they take part in 'amorous jousts', they should be pardoned. Other men and women, at the bottom of the social hierarchy, are excluded from the game because they are too base. This includes prostitutes: they sell themselves, and expect a wage. It includes all manual workers, the country people and towns-people whom Andrew calls 'peasants' (*rustici*), translating into Latin the romance word he has in mind, the word *vilain*.

Vile, they are incapable of fine love. The rational soul (*anima rationalis*) is too weak and too clumsy to restrain, as it ought, the stirrings of the flesh. For them, love was indistinguishable from toil. These peasants did it like animals. To love honourably requires, first, total gratuitousness and disinterestedness. So much so that, for Andrew, the woman who accepts anything other than trinkets, or the ribbons and flounces that increased her attractions and reminded her of her lover, ranked among the whores; better go to the real thing, they were cheaper. To love 'honourably' also required leisure, *otium*, and those graces of the body that physical labour destroyed and that were the prerogative of men who had nothing to do but play. They alone had the right to enter the arena. This did not, of course, preclude them from leaving it to pursue their quarry elsewhere. If a woman of the people pleased them, let them enjoy her in passing, but without preliminaries, without preparing their approach; she did not deserve it. 'If by chance, peasant women attract you, be careful to flatter them . . . if you find the occasion favourable, do not hesitate to satisfy your desire, take them by force . . . you have to compel them and cure them of their modesty.' There was no achievement here, of course, nor glory. But such outbursts in men should be tolerated; they take everything that comes within their reach. It is their nature. The clergy, everybody knows, run after girls. The man of quality, the man of leisure, does not disdain violent, bestial love in the manner of peasants.

Nevertheless, if he wished to raise himself, to increase in valour through the proper use of his virility, it was better to remain in his own world, which was that of the court. It was here that love was king, bore a crown and distributed the prizes. Did Andrew not call 'courtesy' all the good of which it was the source? But at the end of the twelfth century, court society was complex. Men – and married women, since they bore their husband's title and shared his privileges – were divided into three ranks. At the lowest level were those who were only really at leisure on Sundays and feast days, who, the rest of the time, practised *negotium*. They were men of affairs, money men, whom the prince had only recently admitted into his entourage. Andrew sought a Latin word to indicate them, and chose *plebeius*. The classical texts used this word for men of lesser rank who, though citizens, nevertheless ranked far above the populace. A clear boundary separated them from the nobles; nobility was a matter of birth and implied complete personal freedom. Within it, he distinguished two degrees. Above the *nobilis* were the *nobilior*, the more noble. This hierarchy was much firmer then it appeared, and necessarily so. The layers of honours, the rules of precedence and the susceptibilities to which they gave rise were all turned to his advantage by the prince, always anxious to avoid trouble within his house. Further, among the laws of the game of love, those that required a scrupulous respect for rank were by no means the least strict. *Honestas* consisted also of knowing one's place. The *De amore* reminds the reader of this. A man was permitted to be first to greet a lady. 'If he has by his rank more privileges than she, he may sit down beside her without seeking her permission; if he is of the same rank, he seeks her permission and, with her agreement, sits down beside her, but never without. When the man is of lower rank . . . he must seek to sit below her. However, if she permits him, he may sit by her side.' These were not trivialities, but the rules of etiquette. Such an order did nothing, nevertheless, to restrain the spirit of adventure. As long as he respected the forms, every member of the 'knighthood of lovers' was free to try his luck. As at a tournament, irrespective of title, the best man won. Everybody competed for the booty, that is, for the ladies, all the ladies of the court. So the commoner might look very far above him, and assail even the highest noblewoman, daring to seek her favours. Would she give in? Why not? Andrew watched the game. What did he teach his pupil Walter?

It is by no means easy to decide, since the *De amore* is, for us, a difficult text, as the flood of conflicting scholarly commentaries devoted to it over the decades testifies. Andrew did not, it appears, compose it 'under the inspiration of Marie of Champagne', as many still claim. Nor is it, in spite of the title given to it by its editor and French translator,

Claude Buridant, a 'treatise on courtly love'. It is concerned
with sexual morality, showing that it is possible to transmute
into virtue the violent impulses of the flesh. It sets out to
prove this by means with which we are unfamiliar. To
disentangle the propositions which are interwoven throughout this book, and explain their significance, we would need
to be able to think as a Parisian intellectual who was
contemporary with Philip Augustus thought, to know everything that he knew and only what he knew, to organize our
concepts in the way he did, and to combine as he did rational
deductions and verbal associations. The author presents
himself as a *magister*, and writes in the Latin of the schools,
the best schools, where he had been taught. He wrote for his
peers and his friends, the clergy of the court. He wrote also
for the increasingly large body of 'literate knights' who were
employed by the king and who were capable of understanding his language. He was counting on them to disseminate
what he said throughout the court society he aimed to
enlighten and make more moral. If he chose to contain his
discourse within a dry scholasticism, it was perhaps so that
the extremely subversive ideas that he was daring to express
would not be condemned out of hand, and so that his book,
instead of being burned, would be respectfully preserved in
the Treasury of charters.

Andrew was a fount of knowledge. He knew everything
that was then known about handling words, about the
harmonies of the world, about medicine, law, the two laws,
canon and Roman, as they were taught in the Paris of his
day. He was equipped with all the baggage necessary to
anyone who wished to engage in the study of the sacred, of
God and theology. He remained, however, *in mundo*, in the
earthly world, but it was a terrain he had explored from top
to bottom. The reader of today does not know, however,
and it is this that is so disconcerting, that it is necessary to
place behind each of his assertions whichever part of this
immense learning supported and shed light on it. No less
disconcerting are his methods of exposition, for example the
way that, when he discusses a 'question', he defends with
equal vigour an argument in favour and its opposite, or the

multiple meanings with which the terms he employs are invested. No one can be confident they appreciate them all. Lastly, we have to allow for the irony. Drouart la Vache, who translated the treatise into Romance a century after it was written, and who was better placed than we are to catch its true tone, says in his preface that, reading it, he doubled up with laughter. But where does the joke begin? And where does it end? As unqualified as the next person, I believe I can distinguish in this great, superabundant book, three closely connected projects.

One is obvious: Andrew wanted to write a manual, an 'art' as he put it, of seduction. To increase his value, the knight of love must conquer women. Andrew taught him how, *ingeniosus*, to set the trap (*engigner*) that would catch them, how to attract (*allicere*) them to him and, one by one, overcome their defences by confusing them with words. Eloquence, skill in persuading and in refuting the arguments of an opponent, was one of the essential values of chivalric culture. As soon as the man of war ceased to seek to vanquish by the sword, he talked, and he set out to shine in conversation by his fluency and the sharpness of his repartee. When Henry I of England wanted to test the valour of Geoffrey Plantagenet, to whom he was planning to give his daughter, he made him sit down beside him and engaged him in conversation, obliging him to give proof of his loquacity. The *De amore* includes eight models of amorous discourse. They account for a large part of the work and take pride of place at its centre. Andrew presents six people, two by two and face to face, three men and three women, from the three levels of courtly society. He has them debate, thus making the reader climb with them the rungs of the ladder of honours, and also that of the values of love. The *plebeius* begins, speaking first to his equal, then to the two women who are above him. Next comes the turn of the *nobilis*; he speaks to the noble lady, then to the most noble. The *nobilior*, lastly, makes his appearance. Starting from the bottom, he engages in conversation successively with each of the three women. The movement is upwards, which is that of all progress in art, and that of all apprenticeship.

Dialogues are by no means rare in the writings of the twelfth century. Every advance in scholastic thinking proceeded from a 'dispute', a linguistic battle, and pedagogic works often took the form of a conversation between the master and his disciple. The letters of Héloïse and Abelard respond one to the other. In romances, as in pastorales, the plot progressed through an exchange of words. In Latin scholarly literature, however, Andrew the Chaplain is the first to build his proof not, admittedly, on controversy, but on a series of encounters, face to face, between a man and a woman. They are of equal power, a remarkable innovation, a sign of the changes taking place in relations between the two sexes in the high society of the period. Masculine and feminine, two opposing principles, confront each other. The man always attacks, which is his function; he is like the hunter, or like the knight who, in the crush of the tournament, marks down the opponent he aims to put to ransom, heads straight for his prey, gathers speed and charges, lance couched. This treatise on honourable love advises him, nevertheless, to be cautious and to weigh his words carefully. One must be wary of women; they know how to wrong-foot an aggressor and 'ridicule him by cutting words'. Little by little, he will gain ground. The female principle, in contrast, is conservative ('Women are conservative; they desire solidity', Michelet could still write in 1859). Women, guardians of stability, resist, they call to order, which is necessary, and they warn against leaving the rank that the heart and the body assign. ('You are brave', they say to one man, 'but you are not well born.' To another, 'It is not because you are of good blood that you show so much virtue.') The pursuer argues and speaks reason, but he ought also to fan the flames. This is what the *plebeia* retorts to the high noble who presses her: where is the *trait*, the arrow, where is the wound? Can she rely on the favours of the king of Love if she is not overcome by 'the feelings by which the heart is moved'? Eroticism should not be icy or cerebral; without emotion, there is no happiness in love. Women riposte and parry blows, which they do with great elegance. The discourse attributed to them by Andrew the Chaplain is evidence of the esteem in which he held them. They are astute, skilful in discussion, they, too, use irony and they are in no way inferior to men in their use of language. The image of women and of courtesy offered by this cleric is remarkable for its brilliance and its subtlety, which is itself of considerable importance. Nevertheless, when they, in their turn, have raised their value by refusing themselves, then no longer refusing entirely while managing to avoid disorder, women surrender. Their role is to yield and so they must decline in honour.

A man and a woman talk together. When they are of the same rank, it is the man who guides and who expounds the rules of the game. The male commoner reminds the female commoner that 'there is no greater gift for a woman than to submit totally to the dominion of another'. She will give herself, there is no doubt. But she should hold back, and should know how to prolong the pleasure of anticipation, be neither too easy nor too modest. The nobleman recommends the same attitude to the woman who is his equal, justifying it by an allegory. He describes the 'palace of love' as it appeared one day to the astonished eyes of a young squire of Robert of Dreux. The boy was hunting in the 'royal forest of France'. At a distance, in a large clearing, he spied a sizable mounted company, led by a man who wore a crown. He approached, and saw that a company of very elegantly dressed women headed the procession. Their horses were spirited and they ambled along in good order, each escorted by three knights. Other women followed, but in disorder, and they were being harassed by all sorts of men on foot. There followed a last company, made up of women who were 'vile and abject', riding nags, in a cloud of dust. They were very beautiful, but badly dressed, oppressed by the heat under the fox skins that weighed them down. The young man stopped one of them and questioned her. What you see, she told him, is an army of the dead. One day a week, love, 'who rules the whole world and without whom no one can do good on earth', takes the head of the procession. He has judged each of these women and, according to their merits, divided them into three cohorts. He is leading the first into the centre of an enclosed garden, under the great tree of life, into the cool of its shade, by live fountains; there, beds are prepared, and they are surrounded by musicians. They have the right to this tranquil happiness because they have behaved 'prudently', granting their favours to the men whose valour they were capable of appreciating. Shameless and depraved, the women of the second company have given themselves to all sorts of lovers, without discrimination and without moderation. Icy streams which overflow run through the second circle, to which they are confined, under a fierce sun. In the third, which is equally torrid, seats of thorns await those most severely punished, those who have been too surly and impervious, who have refused the service of love.

The lesson is clear. The man has started the hare and he is enjoying the chase. The more the prey he hunts is skilled at evasion, the greater his pleasure. But this pleasure culminates in the capture. At this point, the question arises as to whether this treatise, which teaches how to seduce, aims also to show how to enjoy the seduction? Is this manual for the seducer also a manual of eroticism? Should it, as Betsy Bowden has suggested, be called *A Treatise on Courtly Copulation*? In favour of giving it such a title are all the words with double or even triple meanings, the puns, the incongruous consonances and those innocent Latin terms that suggested to anyone who spoke them aloud extremely ribald Romance words, everything that made Drouart roar with laughter. I want, rather, to emphasize two points. In the last of the eight dialogues, at the end of the upward journey, the man and the woman of the upper nobility, in the perfect freedom conferred by their high birth, discuss love. He bows down before the woman and does homage to her power. Is this irony, the final manoeuvre, the man pretending to abase himself in order to undermine the last rampart? Or is it an assertion that, in its most refined forms, love, like good friendship, abolishes the hierarchies? The couple discuss the stain that, if one plays the game right to the end, risks sullying the most pure, the clergy and above all, the marriageable daughters.

We need to distinguish, says the great lord, between *amor mixtus* (how should this be translated? Surely not, like Buridan, by 'physical love'. I myself suggest 'mixed love', that is, imperfect, troubled love) and *amor purus* (the translation here is clear, it is *fin'amor*, fine love). 'This love [pure love] joins hearts . . . with all the power of passion. It consists of the contemplation of the mind and the feelings of the heart. It goes as far as kissing on the mouth, embraces and chaste contact with the naked body of the beloved. The ultimate pleasure, however, is excluded.' We recognize here the 'test', the dream extolled by some of the troubadours, but situated always in an improbable future, like a mirage, inaccessible, the body of the mistress finally unclothed, fully offered and appreciated, but respected. Of course, it is the man who is speaking here and who is continuing his offensive. Is he not promising the woman he seeks to capture that he will stop there, at this test, this exploit? He adds that pure love 'never ceases to grow in strength', and is all the more fevered the more that desire is prolonged, whereas the other love fades as soon as the fruit is plucked. But his partner counter-attacks with a question she poses in the manner of an expert dialectician. There was once, she says, a lady who was courted by two suitors. She made them a proposition: 'Let one of you choose the top half of my body, and the other will have the lower half.' Which of them gets the better part? At this point, the debate takes a new turn. The man and woman from the highest nobility are very obviously having fun. She plays devil's advocate, and claims that the greatest pleasure is taken below the belt and that it is in these parts, consequently, that love reaches its fulfilment. He counters that, throughout the whole of the universe, the upper is always superior to the lower, hence 'logical order demands that one obtain first, after many entreaties, the lovely pleasures of the upper part in order next, and only then, and gradually, to reach the others'. For, if fine love is superior in quality, mixed love is not without its charms. Why deprive oneself of it, since 'one can purge by a simple penance what one does from a natural impulse?' Nature is once again evoked, not only to exonerate, but also to induce one to savour the pleasures more, by dint of restraint and by controlling one's desire right to the end.

I note also the arguments of Danielle Jacquart and Claude Thomasset. On the basis of a very close scrutiny of the Latin words, and by comparing them with the Romance terms used by Drouart to translate them, they claim to have discovered, under cover of the scholastic arguments, a mass of practical advice teaching the techniques of the embrace by which one could avoid the disastrous consequences of adultery or of the defloration of virgins. Was it not essential to preserve the social order, not to produce bastards and therefore not to impregnate one's partner in pleasure? Pleasure, too, was all-important. Is it diminished when one knows how to remain in full control of one's body and one's mind?

We must be careful not to take everything we find in this treatise too seriously. But to look no further than the jokes and the erotic subtleties would be to err in a different way. This book, and this is its third theme, prescribes a strict morality for the benefit of the *curiales*. Let us play at love among ourselves, while we are young, and sheltered by the barrier that separates us from the peasantry. We will enjoy ourselves very much. But we will also learn how to master our lusts, thereby preparing ourselves, *cupiditas* commuted into *caritas*, to come closer to the love of God. In essence, the project of Andrew the Chaplain is perhaps not so very different from that of Bernard of Clairvaux. Simply, he starts from the very bottom, remains at the level of the carnal and does not venture outside the 'world'. His work was timely. It aimed to reply to one of the questions being posed in Paris in the last decades of the twelfth century, in response to the consequences of the general progress. Not far away, in the cloister of Notre-Dame, Peter the Chanter and his disciples were asking what was to be done about power, the pervasive power of the king, of his judges and of his tax-collectors, and what was to be done about money, which it was clear was penetrating everywhere and disturbing everything. Round the young king, Andrew saw more and more women. The court of France, which in the previous reign had been packed with monks and priests, and saturated with liturgy, was now wide open to the fashions that were being propagated from the courts of princes by the successful songs and romances. What was to be done about women? What was to be done about the new love?

This new love, it was said, could only flourish outside marriage. This was the opinion of the man from the higher nobility. The noble lady he was making up to objected: 'I have a husband, he is courteous and virtuous; it would be a crime to defile his bed. All the more so, since he loves me with all his heart and I am deeply attached to him.' His reply was: How can you 'use the word love for the sentiment that husband and wife are supposed to feel for each other when they are joined in marriage? We all know that love cannot exist between them', since they are bound by a contract, and since this contract requires that they cherish each other and sleep together. Love can only be free. Besides, that 'frantic desire passionately to enjoy furtive and secret embraces', how could it exist within the conjugal union, where the communion of bodies is lawful? Without danger, there is no prowess. The lady reasonably and rationally asks in reply why there cannot be secret embraces between spouses, and transports, and ardour. Cannot the man she has chosen be both husband and lover? But this is impossible. If, in marriage, pleasure exceeds 'that which derives from the desire to procreate or from the discharge of the debt', there is an offence, and a grave one, 'because to abuse something sacred is to profane it'. And to conclude the debate, the *nobilior* quotes from a letter from Marie of Champagne. This was a complete fabrication. Maliciously, Andrew dated it to 1 May, the feast of love, and to 1174, the year in which Chrétien de Troyes wrote *Lancelot*. 'Love', the countess is supposed to have said, 'cannot extend its sway over spouses. For lovers give each other everything freely, not bound by any obligation. Whereas a married couple is bound by duty to comply with each other's desires and may in no circumstances refuse each other.' It is a question of distinction: 'Do the spouses have more if they embrace each other like lovers?

Their merit is not increased and they apparently have nothing more than they had by right before.' There exist, then, two ways of sleeping together and of taking pleasure together, one within marriage, the other outside; on the one hand, duty, security and affection, on the other, gratuitousness, hardship, peril and what one is entitled to call love.

Andrew the Chaplain was mocking courtly love as it was described in the profane literature he knew so well. In his references to the game of love as extolled by the troubadours, with its pettifoggery and its preciosity, all is parody, and the sentences he concocted and attributed to the princesses of the Midi, Eleanor of Aquitaine and Ermengarde of Narbonne, are risible. His real intention, as Rüdiger Schnell perceived, was to show, by pushing the dictates of imaginary courts of love to absurd lengths, and by treating the code of courtly love in the same way that the moralists in the schools treated the laws of marriage, that in the last analysis the two systems imposed analogous constraints on the couple and that a similar status was assigned to the woman in both. She was no less subject, exploited or dominated in free love than in marriage. As a result, the sphere of 'honourable' love was enlarged, opened up to the whole of court society. The man of the highest nobility, in the same dialogue, pretends to assume all the roles. I am a cleric, he says, then, a little later, I am a married man. 'You must', his partner in the dialogue replies, 'be a prisoner of your carnal desire for you not to be content with your wife. She is so beautiful.' He says in reply: 'My wife is beautiful, it is true, and I feel for her all the affection [he chooses his word carefully] that a husband can feel', but love is a different quality and I do not seek only to satisfy my desire. It is the same with young girls, he goes on. They have the right to enrol in the militia of King Love. Before they marry, it is a good thing for them to love. With reference to Iseult, Blanchefleur and Fenice, he says: 'If a young girl does not seek to advance her fame through the power of love, she does not deserve to receive a husband worthy of esteem.'

For practice in love serves to train women as well as men. This is the last and most powerful lesson of the treatise. It lays down a collection of rules adapted to the female nature, which should lead women to surpass themselves, and should make them, too, become 'valiant knights'. These are the wise and prudent women, those who are able to suppress their taste for behaving like men, for being as predatory as they are. Honour is due to those who do not give their favours in return for money or costly presents. Honour is due above all to those who are cautious, who freely, and 'after mature consideration', choose one partner, and only one, a man they have put to the test and know will be a *sapiens et ingeniosus amator*, that he will restrain himself at the right moment. They are attractive, of course, not voracious, constant, becoming attached to the one their heart has chosen. Andrew imagines a sort of jury composed of the worthiest of women, presided over by the wife of the prince. They would have total power, wisely distributing blame and praise, to exclude and relegate to infamy those of their peers who do not control themselves, giving themselves too quickly or stubbornly resisting. In this way, women would be disciplined, supple mounts, vigorous and docile, tamed for the pleasure of men.

It is a deeply misogynistic treatise. The most convincing expression of its contempt for femininity is not contained in the exaggerated invective that Andrew trots out, following so many others, in the *reprobatio amoris* with which the work ends. He repeats, of course, that 'all women', even queens, were good for nothing, that no man 'was powerful enough to satiate by any means the lust of any woman', and that 'no woman returns a man's love'. The misogyny is cruder in the condescension that grants the women of the court a few derisory prerogatives, the right to allow or not allow the suitor a chance to speak, and to crown the most agreeable of them with flowers. To banish the power of women to the realms of a game where nothing mattered, except a respect for good manners and knowing how to behave, to sit and to turn phrases, was to curb and stifle it, and to diminish the fear of women in the minds of men. The insignificant power men allowed women over trivialities reassured them. Trapped in the twists and turns of amorous casuistry, women would do less harm. In this way, too, the game of love contributed to social peace. For what really mattered was that women should be 'mastered and guided', as is said of the good war horse in all the equine metaphors with which the *De amore* is peppered.

This is a book that confirmed men in their conviction that women were a race apart, and hostile. It convinced them, first, that this disparity was in accord with the laws of nature, hence just. So with regard to the young girl, who was ready for love some time before the young boy, it says: 'It is at the onset of puberty that constancy is most firmly assured, and that she is unlikely to change [so she will not be flighty], so nature has enabled her to perform the act of love earlier than men [hence to become attached to her husband very early, when, in her still soft flesh, the bond can be closely and durably rooted] and this [that is, as a result of physical conditions alone] because women are ruled by a frigid temperament whereas men are inhabited by a natural warmth.' The treatise also persuaded them never to weaken before this enemy, never to trust in her surface sweetness, and to keep her in the condition of object, subject to male power in love as in marriage. The knights wanted the impossible, both that the wives and mistresses of other men would not refuse them and that their own would be faithful. The ambivalent morality of the *De amore* attempted to respond to this dual expectation. It confirmed, at all events, men's certainty that they themselves were absolutely free to act. Was a wife permitted to share herself between two lovers? Of course not. 'This is tolerated among men because it is their habit and because it is a privilege of their sex to perform readily what, in this world, is dishonest by nature. But in a woman, the modesty required by the reserve of her sex renders such behaviour so culpable that after having given herself to many men, she is unworthy to be admitted to the company of wives.' There were two species, and tolerance towards one, the active one, but repression and inexorable domination for the other, the passive one.

The book argued for the utility of love. The discipline it imposed was deemed to make women gracious, desirable, subtle, as discreet as they were welcoming, and capable of giving themselves without betraying their husband. This was the dream. Whereas men, their youth behind them, now well able 'to manage their horse', proud of their victories, no longer amused by the game, emerged from it mature, blasé and ready to consider the safety of their soul. At this point, Andrew withdrew, handing over to the theologians.

Andrew the Chaplain was a keen observer of nature, the nature of things, and human nature. He viewed things by the light of reason. He believed that he understood women. But is the image of them he presents any more accurate than the others I have been trying, in these three books, to recover? Andrew was not, like so many priests, blinded by the prejudices of his order. He made an effort to look at women through the eyes of the novice knight he was pretending to instruct. But, like the young Walter, he was on the defensive. What distorted his vision was the disquiet, the malaise before the female body that men tried to overcome in two ways, by bawdy jokes or by transposing it into unreality, 'the two alternating faces', according to Henri Rey-Flaud, 'of a fundamentally equivocal attitude'. These two attitudes coexisted in the songs attributed to William of Aquitaine: either, as in the fifth, they make the woman's body into a punch bag, rain blows on, beat and wound with every variety of male violence this wicked, adulterous, greedy and deceitful flesh, or they distance it, as in the fourth song, lose it in vagueness and uncertainty ('I have a mistress but I don't know who'), reduce it to nothingness, to rightlessness. A hundred years later, this equivocation found very clear expression in the most popular literary works of the early thirteenth century.

The romances of Jean Renart, for example, present women as they are – as adventuresses. Alice, the heroine of *L'Escoufle*, is single, a strong woman, who earns a good living by being very indulgent to men, a hairdresser and a purveyor of fashion in the shop she had opened in Montpellier, on the borderline between courtesy and high-class prostitution. She is strong, above all, through the tie that binds her to other women, through love, true love, the only one to count in their eyes. She was loved by Isabella, in whose house she lived in Toul and whose bed she shared every night, and by the chatelaine of Montpellier, who wanted to attract her into her own. But she refused, because, like good courtly lovers, she did not share her favours. This is how the enemy is presented, formidable, thanks to the solidarity that binds women closely together and is reinforced by their mutual caresses. But it is precisely this failing, this ardour and their passion for pleasure, that makes it possible to get the better of them. Luckily, they are mostly bisexual. Let us, therefore, cash in. 'Knights, at the ladies!', is the battle-cry of the hero of *Guillaume de Dole*, a 'young' prince, surrounded by 'young men'. In the meadow, under the warm Whitsuntide sun, there were women waiting. They are free, on offer, their husbands far away, out hunting, they said, without anyone being taken in. They held out their arms to the young men, who carried them, submissive, willingly defeated, into the tents, and went from one to the other. 'All the joy in the world was there.'

Those who were worried about sin and the torments promised to the lustful, or were growing old, or were in thrall to their confessor, sought safety in devotion, orienting their desire in other directions, towards images and towards other women whose tokens of affection, dispensed in the hereafter, proved without danger and beneficial. Easily the most attractive of them was Our Lady. Her cult, which had been growing since the Carolingian period, had swept through Christendom like a torrent since the end of the eleventh century, since St Anselm had seen in the Mother of God the new Eve, the anti-Eve: EVA reversed to make AVE. There were pilgrimages and miracles, and women rushed to the relics, not the remains of her body, which the angels had raised to the highest part of Heaven, but the clothes she had worn, her shift, deposited by Charles the Bald at Chartres, the shoe preserved at Soissons, a few drops of her milk, etc. etc. And men, too, were converted, aspiring to union and to love. At the beginning of the twelfth century, the canons of Utrecht denounced a heretic called Tanchelm to the archbishop of Cologne. Like his contemporary, Robert of Arbris-

sel, he had a following of women in search of spiritual
comfort and, according to his accusers, had publicly celebrated his marriage to the Virgin. One day, 'he gave orders
for an image of St Mary to be brought into the middle of the
crowd; stepping forward, he placed his hand in the hand of
the statue and, in this way, he married St Mary. He pro-
nounced with his sacrilegious mouth the oath and all the
solemn words of marriage.' How many monks and priests
and how many knights dreamed, in the secrecy of their
hearts, of a similar mystical alliance, and of protecting
themselves in this manner from the great sin, the sexual act?
'Honour and cherish Mary. Venerate her, praise her, seek to
please her ... taste the delicious pleasures of her sweetest
love' were the words used by Abbot Adam of Perseigne in
one of his letters to exhort an adolescent boy – that is to say,
all adolescent boys – to serve Our Lady, as the courtly lover
served his mistress. The developing bodies of these young
men were on fire; they were more threatened than most by
sin. They must defend themselves. 'It is easy for those who
are filled with the love of our Virgin ... take her for mother,
for nurse, for wife, for mistress.' Adam concluded: 'She will
never fail you if you love her with love, if you dedicate your
body to her.' They were to give their body, as in marriage,
and so as to deliver it from evil.

As widely known and enjoyed as the romances of Jean
Renart was the *Miracles de Notre-Dame* of Gautier de
Coincy. A monk from the age of fifteen in the abbey of Saint-
Médard, in Soissons, where the members of his family had
their place reserved, he composed this sequence of songs
between 1218 and 1230, in the language of the court. Hating
the Jews and despising the peasantry, he was the perfect
representative of the established, arrogant and dominant
Church. He would have been perfectly happy in the tranquil
material and intellectual comfort amongst which he lived,
without the goad that tormented his flesh, evil desires, 'bitter,
poisoned love', the love 'that stinks'. Happily, he had female
friends to protect him from going astray. I do not refer to
princesses, or the good sisters of Notre-Dame of Soissons,
the custodians of Our Lady's shoe. I refer to Leocadia, virgin

and martyr. When he had been in charge of the priory of
Vic-sur-Aisne, Walter had watched over her body; she was
his 'lady love'. I refer, above all, to the Virgin Mary. Walter
sang her praises, in all registers, and with considerable skill.
Throughout the century, theologians had struggled hard and
long to discover the features that distinguished the body of
the Mother of God from all other female bodies. (When she
had brought the son of God into the world, the door of her
womb had remained mysteriously closed. Had she ever, like
other women, been sullied by menstrual blood? Had she not
been alone among human beings to escape original sin? And
the idea of celebrating her immaculate conception had
already emerged by 1140.) In this sequence of unsophisti-
cated little stories put into agreeable verse, however, Mary
remains very much a woman. She was seductive, to the point
of dazzling the devil when he appeared to him at night, 'in
a very ornate shift', displaying the splendours of her flowing
hair. What attracted Walter was her bosom, her breasts, the
little breasts 'that are so soft and round and lovely'. He
served her, and he called on others to serve her, loyally,
assiduously, and with a fine love. She was generous to all
who loved her. But she was also jealous. Her wrath
descended on any man who dared to neglect her. She
suddenly appeared on the wedding night, and placed herself
between the bridegroom who had betrayed her and the
fiancée he was preparing to enjoy. 'You have rejected me, do
you find her better or more beautiful than I?' It was Mary,
of course, who won. Bearing no grudge, she granted the
repentant lover what she had promised him, 'joy, solace and
company'. In Paradise, in her bedchamber, he would soon
join her. Her servants had orders to prepare the bed. Our
Lady would leave the heart to her son, but she would keep
the body. Was this *amor purus*, or was it, sublimated,
admittedly, and immaculate, but with a strong streak of
sensuality, *amor mixtus*?

Conclusion

S ome fifteen years ago, at the very end of my book, *The Knight, the Lady and the Priest*, I posed the question: how much do we really know about women? Since then I have been searching among all the traces left by the women of the twelfth century. I had become fond of them. I knew very well that I would see nothing of their faces, their gestures or their way of dancing or laughing, but I hoped to catch sight of some aspects of the way they behaved, and of how they saw themselves, the world and men. I have glimpsed only fleeting, elusive shadows. None of their words has survived. All the speech that was attributed to them at the time is masculine.

I can imagine them, at least, on their own territory, beneath the veils in which male authority enveloped them, inside the walls within which it wished to keep them confined, and behind the screen that is erected before the historian's eyes by the invective and the contempt of men; I imagine them to be solidly united by the secrets they transmitted among themselves and by forms of love comparable to those that, at this period, gave cohesion to military companies; I imagine them as invested with great power — over the domestic servants through their position as wives, over their children through maternity, and over the knights who surrounded them through their culture, their charms and the relations they were believed to cultivate with the invisible powers; I imagine them to be strong, much stronger than I used to think, and even happy, so strong that men tried hard to weaken them by the anguish of sin. Also, it seems to me that one can situate around 1180, when the violent surge of growth sweeping through Europe was at its height, the time when the situation of these women was a little improved, when men became accustomed to treating them as persons, to negotiating with them, to enlarging their sphere of freedom, and to cultivating those special gifts that made them closer to the supernatural. This is the main conclusion to emerge from my research.

Lastly, I know more about the men who were their contemporaries, and about how they saw women. Eve both attracted them and frightened them. Either they kept a prudent distance from women, or else they treated them roughly, mocking them, entrenched in the stubborn conviction of their natural superiority. It was men, ultimately, who failed women.